The
HOLIDAY
HANDBOOK

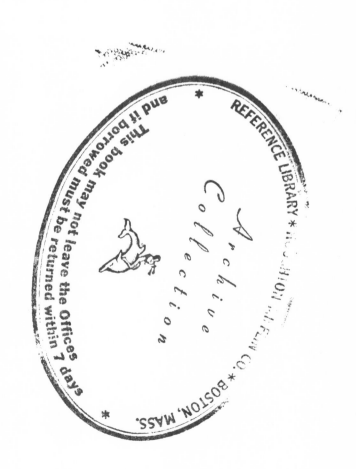

The HOLIDAY HANDBOOK

by *Carol Barkin*
and Elizabeth James

Illustrations by Melanie Marder Parks

CLARION BOOKS

New York

Clarion Books
a Houghton Mifflin Company imprint
215 Park Avenue South, New York, NY 10003
Text copyright © 1994 by Carol Barkin and Elizabeth James
Illustrations copyright © 1994 by Melanie Marder Parks
Type is 11/14 pt. New Aster.
Printed in the USA.

Library of Congress Cataloging-in-Publication Data
Barkin, Carol.
  The holiday handbook / by Carol Barkin and Elizabeth James.
    p. cm.
  Summary: A handbook of secular holidays, arranged by season,
describing their origins, ways to celebrate them, and other
pertinent facts.
  ISBN 0-395-65011-9   PA ISBN 0-395-67888-9
  1. Holidays—United States—Juvenile literature. 2. Holidays—Juvenile literature. [1. Holidays.] I. James, Elizabeth. II. Title.
GT4803.B37   1993
394.2'6—dc20   92-29846
                                                 CIP
                                                 AC

VB   10 9 8 7 6 5 4 3 2 1

For David, Katie, Drew, Brian, Daniel,
Matthew, and Jennifer
—C.B.

In loving memory of my mom,
Sally L. James
—E.J.

Acknowledgments

We'd like to thank all the people who helped us by providing information or encouragement, or both, while we wrote this book. Special thanks go to June Otani Baensch, Naomi Caldwell-Wood, Farhad Ebrahimi, the Reverend Joseph Gilmore, Usha Jain, Angelo Joaquin, Jr., of the Tohono O'odham Nation, Kitty Nakagawa, and Rabbi Edward Schecter. Many thanks too to the organizations that sent us materials on various holidays; in addition to those listed in the Appendix, they include American Indian Culture Research Center, Council for Indian Education, and Inter-Tribal Indian Ceremonial Association. We're grateful to the authors of all the books we consulted on holidays and how they are celebrated and on topics connected with the holidays; in the course of our research we discovered vast amounts of fascinating and useful information that helped us refine our own ideas. Finally, we want to express our heartfelt gratitude to our editors at Clarion Books, Dorothy Briley and Dinah Stevenson, without whose insight and patience this book would never have seen the light of day.

Contents

WINTER

SPRING

SUMMER

Introduction

Holidays are meant to be celebrated. They give you a chance to have fun, spend time with friends and family, and get out of your day-to-day routine.

There's something special about every holiday, something that sets it apart from ordinary days and makes it unique. Some holidays honor a particular person, such as Johnny Appleseed or Martin Luther King, Jr., who made an important contribution to the world. Others celebrate a whole group of people—mothers, for instance, or presidents—and still others, such as Veterans Day and Independence Day, commemorate historical events. There are holidays that remind us to think about our ideals for ourselves and the world: World Food Day, Earth Day, and Thanksgiving are all times to focus on ideas that are meaningful to us. Traditional holidays that have been celebrated for centuries include Halloween and New Year's Day. And besides all these, there are holidays such as National Grouch Day and International Left-handers Day that people have invented just because they thought it would be fun.

But how did the idea of holidays get started in the first place? Many people believe that the earliest holidays were connected with the seasons of the year and with religious beliefs. In fact, our word *holiday* comes from Old English words that mean "holy day." Ancient peoples had only the crops they grew or the animals they hunted to eat. If rain didn't fall and the crops didn't grow, or if game animals were driven away by drought or fires, people would starve. Each culture believed in gods or spirits who controlled the world and everything that happened in it. Special days were set aside to ask the gods and spirits for rain and sun at planting time and to give thanks for good harvests.

Some elements of the old religions continued, becoming intertwined with new religions as they developed. For example, it's interesting to discover that quite a few of today's major religious holidays occur in spring and fall—planting and harvest seasons. And religious calendars for the most part are based on the cycles of the moon. This means that many religious holidays fall on different dates each year, because the lunar calendar doesn't match up exactly with the calendar we use in daily life.

Whole books have been written about the many religions that are observed all over the world and the different ways their holidays are celebrated. While this book focuses on secular (nonreligious) holidays, it provides brief descriptions of the major world religions and their holidays. As you read about them, take the opportunity to talk with your friends and relatives. What special meanings and customs do they associate with these holidays? You may discover that your grandparents brought holiday traditions with them when they came to the United States. Or perhaps a friend from another part of the country celebrates religious holidays differently from the way you do. In your class there are probably kids from different religious backgrounds, and it's fun to share these important parts of your lives with one another.

Of course, there are also lots of secular holidays that couldn't be part of this book—if all the holidays people celebrate were included, the book would be too heavy to lift!

Some popular holidays occur on different dates in different parts of the United States: Arbor Day, for example, is celebrated at various times during the spring, and since this book is arranged by holiday dates, it would be too confusing to include holidays that have many different dates.

The holidays we've included are spread all through the year, so there's always something to look forward to. Lots of them are well known, but you've probably never heard of others. For each one, you'll find some fascinating facts about how it got started and unusual projects to do on your own or with a group.

Now's your chance to pick out a new holiday to celebrate, or to discover some new ways of celebrating your old favorites. You might even start at the beginning of the fall and celebrate everything right through to the end of the summer. Or try adapting a project from one holiday to create your own style of celebrating a different one. Whatever you decide, you'll be amazed at the tremendous variety of holidays in the United States and the wealth of ways they can be celebrated. Have fun, and happy holidays!

Presenting Fall

In the Northern Hemisphere, fall officially begins on the day of the autumnal equinox, which occurs sometime around September 22 each year. There are two equinoxes every year, fall and spring. They are the points in the earth's revolution around the sun when the sun seems to cross the Equator; at these two times in the year, day and night are of equal length everywhere in the world.

Fall means harvest time, the season when crops are gathered and stored for the winter ahead. In some cultures this is the end of the old year and the beginning of a new one. For many people it is a time to give thanks according to their own religious practices.

In many parts of Asia, a harvest festival is celebrated on the fifteenth day of the eighth month of the Asian lunar year (September or October). In China it is often called Harvest Moon, while in Japan it is Obon and in Korea it is called Chusok. People in the United States celebrate this holiday in many cities with street fairs, dancing, costumes, and special foods such as moon cakes.

Hinduism

Fall is an important time of the year for Hindus. Hinduism, which began about 1500 B.C. in India, is the oldest major religion in today's world. More than half a billion people are Hindus. For Hindus, there is no single being called God, as there is in western religions. Instead, the Hindu religion is based on the idea of Brahman—infinite peace and perfection.

The goal of Hindus is to reach and become one with Brahman. This can be achieved through living according to certain ideals, such as purity, truth, and compassion toward all living creatures. Many lifetimes may be needed before a Hindu soul is united with Brahman. Hindus believe that each soul is reborn as many times as necessary to reach a state of purity and perfection.

Many gods and goddesses represent various aspects of the infinite and all-inclusive Brahman. Three major gods are Vishnu the Preserver, Shiva the Destroyer, and Brahma the Creator. But many others are worshiped in Hindu temples. Sacred writings about legendary figures like Rama and Krishna tell stories that help people understand the Hindu view of the world.

Hinduism is not structured the way some other religions are. There is no specific time in the week or year when Hindus are expected to gather in a temple for organized worship together; people go to their temples to pray or make offerings whenever they choose. Much of Hinduism is based on prayers and traditions carried out at home. Also, Hindu spiritual leaders are not in charge of congregations, the way Christian ministers and priests are.

Hinduism was not started by any one person. However, the men who founded several other religions, such as Buddhism, Jainism, and Sikhism, were Hindus who rejected or changed certain aspects of the religion they grew up with. And Hinduism itself has many sects whose religious practices focus on particular gods or goddesses.

Hundreds of Hindu holidays are celebrated every year. On these joyful occasions parades go through the streets with painted elephants and bands with drums and cymbals. Some Hindu festivals are held in only one small village; some are celebrated only by men or by women; some honor several gods and goddesses at the same time. But there are some holidays in the fall that are celebrated by Hindus everywhere.

Durga Puja and Dushera

Two Hindu holidays take place at around the same time; Durga Puja is celebrated mainly by Bengalis in northern areas of India, while Dushera is celebrated by most other Hindus. Durga Puja occurs in September or October (the date varies according to the moon). Durga (also called Kali, Parvati, or Sakti) is the wife of Shiva; *Puja* means "worship." Durga is the mother goddess, and mothers are honored by their families during Durga Puja. This holiday celebrates Durga's victory over the demon king and the return of peace to the world. Small clay or wooden statues of Durga are honored during this time.

Dushera is celebrated at around the same time as Durga Puja. Dushera commemorates the victory of Rama, a legendary hero, over a demon named Ravana. Parts of the Ramayana (the sacred Hindu story of the life of Rama) are performed during the ten-day period of Dushera. People visit their friends and enjoy feasting and dancing.

Diwali

Diwali, the Festival of Lights, begins at dusk on the night of the new moon in late October or early November. Houses and streets are filled with lamps and strings of lights. Young girls have small lamps to float on the river; if her lamp stays alight as long as she can see it, a girl will have good luck in the coming year. Diwali is fun for everyone; fireworks go off, gifts are exchanged, and parties are held everywhere.

Diwali honors Lakshmi, the goddess of good luck and prosperity. Houses are cleaned so Lakshmi will visit them. For businesspeople, Diwali is the beginning of the new year; they pay their debts so they can start fresh. This is also a time to put an end to quarrels and forgive enemies.

Part of the Ramayana is also performed at Diwali. According to the story, Rama had been exiled for fourteen years by his stepmother; during his exile he defeated the demon Ravana. Diwali is the day when Rama returned to his kingdom, and his people celebrated his homecoming with lights.

Judaism

Abraham, whose story is told in the Book of Genesis in the Bible, is considered to be the first Jew. Today there are about 17 million Jews worldwide. The central idea of Judaism is that there is one God and that he is concerned with how people live their lives.

Abraham was one of the first people to believe that there was only one true god. According to Jewish beliefs, God promised Abraham that he and his descendants would be the beginning of a great people if they obeyed God's laws. Abraham's son was Isaac; Isaac's son Jacob had twelve sons, whose descendants became the twelve tribes of Israel.

In the 1200s B.C. (more than three thousand years ago), Moses led the Israelites out of slavery in Egypt. The Torah (Judaism's holy book) says that at Mount Sinai God spoke to Moses and gave him what later became known as the Ten Commandments. This was the beginning of Judaism as an organized religion. The Commandments are rules for living that are basic to Jewish law and belief. They concern people's relationships with their families as well as their neighbors, and they emphasize honesty and honoring both God and other people.

Although Jews believe in an afterlife, the emphasis of Judaism is on living an ethical and virtuous life in this world. Jews look forward to the coming of a Messiah, who will bring all people together under God and give everlasting peace to the world.

While many Jewish religious observances take place at home, Jews worship at synagogues (also called temples); they choose a rabbi, who conducts services and interprets God's laws for the congregation. One of the Ten Commandments instructs people to work for only six days each week; the seventh day is the Sabbath, which is set aside for prayer and rest. In Judaism the Sabbath begins at sundown on Friday and ends at sundown on Saturday.

Judaism spread from the Middle East to many parts of the world, and today it is practiced in different ways. Some Jews strictly follow all the rules and rituals that grew up over the centuries, while others believe in adapting these rules to modern life.

According to tradition, most Jewish holidays celebrate times when God played a direct part in the history of the Jewish people.

Rosh Hashanah and Yom Kippur

One of the most important holidays in Judaism is in the fall, near the autumnal equinox. It is a ten-day holy period that begins with Rosh Hashanah and ends on the day called Yom Kippur. Rosh Hashanah is the Jewish New Year; it is both the day on which the world was created and the Day of Judgment, when God judges each person's life during the past year.

Jewish tradition says that on Rosh Hashanah, God opens three books. In one he inscribes the names of the wicked who will be punished with death; in the second, the Book of Life, he writes the names of righteous people; in the third are written the names of those for whom judgment is not yet made. They will have ten days to repent and atone for their bad deeds.

On Rosh Hashanah Jews go to the synagogue, and the *shofar*, or ram's horn, is sounded to remind people of the trumpet that will blow on the final judgment day. Then for ten days they consider their past sins, repent of the bad things they have done, and ask for God's forgiveness.

Yom Kippur, the Day of Atonement, ends this period of soul-searching. Many Jews fast on Yom Kippur to symbolize their repentance. At sundown the shofar sounds again to end the fast.

Sukkoth

Sukkoth, or the Feast of Tabernacles, is a fall harvest festival, celebrating the gathering of crops. During the eight-day holiday each Jewish family builds a sukkah—a small enclosure, usually outdoors. The sukkah reminds Jews of the shelters (called tabernacles) the Israelites built in the desert after Moses led them out of Egypt. The sukkah is decorated with fruit and flowers, and the family eats its meals there during Sukkoth.

Hanukkah

In December the eight-day festival of Hanukkah is celebrated. More than two thousand years ago the Syrian-Greeks invaded Jerusalem and took over the Jews' holy places. A small army of Jews led by Judah Maccabee defeated the Syrian-Greeks and rededicated the temple in Jerusalem. There was only enough oil to keep the temple's lamp burning for one day. But miraculously, the oil lasted for eight days.

Hanukkah celebrates this victory and miracle. A candleholder called a *hanukkiah* (many people call it a Hanukkah menorah) is used in every home; one candle is lit on the first night of Hanukkah, two on the second night, and so on until eight candles are burning on the last night of the holiday. Games, songs, and gifts, often of money, make this a joyous time for everyone.

October 9

Leif Eriksson Day

Long before Columbus set out from Spain in 1492, other Europeans had "discovered" North America. Many people believe that in the sixth century, an Irish priest named Brendan sailed a small boat from Ireland to Newfoundland, in Canada; there is no proof, though, that this journey actually took place. However, there is lots of evidence that Leif Eriksson, a Norseman who had settled in Greenland, traveled from Greenland to North America sometime between the years 1000 and 1003.

And guess what? Leif Eriksson wasn't the first! He was following the route that another Norse sea captain had taken by accident about fifteen years before. Bjarni Herjolfsson had set out from Iceland to sail to Greenland in the year 985. But north winds and heavy fog drove him off course, and he sailed for many days not knowing where he was. Eventually he sighted land in three different places; however, when the winds finally changed and the fog lifted, Bjarni turned back to Greenland without landing on these unknown shores.

Leif Eriksson, following Bjarni Herjolfsson's directions, landed somewhere in North America in the fall of the year and stayed all winter before returning home. But where did he land? Anywhere from Virginia to Newfoundland, according to people who have studied the evidence.

Archaeologists have found the remains of a Norse settlement at a place called L'Anse aux Meadows in Newfoundland. But they don't agree about whether this is Leif Eriksson's camp or a settlement founded by the Norse explorers who came a few years later. A stone "spindle whorl," used in spinning wool, suggests that women lived at this place, and Leif Eriksson's expedition did not include any women. Still, perhaps one of Leif's sailors carried this spindle as a memento of his wife or sweetheart.

Archaeologists try to find out about the past by digging through the remains of places where people once lived. It's work that takes a long time and a lot of patience, and sometimes the results are hard to interpret. But without archaeology, people might still not know that Norse explorers came to North America nearly five hundred years before Columbus.

Leif Eriksson Day was declared a holiday by a presidential proclamation in 1964, only four years after the first archaeological remains of Norse settlements were found in Canada. Perhaps most people didn't really believe Eriksson had reached these shores until they saw the tools and hearths the archaeologists uncovered.

Did You Know . . . ?

How did people know anything at all about Leif Eriksson before the archaeological discoveries in Canada in 1964? Leif's story, as well as Bjarni Herjolfsson's, was told for many centuries in Scandinavia as part of the sagas that preserved Norse history. The sagas were written down in the 1300s, and a few copies of those handwritten manuscripts are still preserved today in Copenhagen.

But if these stories were not written down until the 1300s, three centuries or more after the Norse explorers reached

North America, how do we know they are true? The answer lies in the writings themselves. The sagas contain many details that we know to be true about North America—so many that it's not possible for someone to have made up these stories. And after all, they were written long before Columbus arrived in America, so the writers could not have heard all these details from him.

Historians have now concluded that for the most part, the ancient sagas that tell of Leif Eriksson's journey to North America are true.

*

Leif Eriksson named the country he found Vinland, which means "wine-land." The saga says that Leif and his men found grapes there, and a German who was with them said that wine could be made from the grapes. Researchers use clues like this to try to figure out where Leif Eriksson actually landed.

But it's not so easy. Grapes can't grow as far north as L'Anse aux Meadows in Newfoundland, so maybe Leif landed farther south. But the saga also mentions salmon that Leif's men caught, and salmon never lived any farther south than Long Island Sound, between New York and Connecticut.

Bits of evidence—such as Norse writing, called runes, cut in stones—have been found in Maine and a few other places. Historians argue about these things and whether they are real or clever fakes, and so far no one has come up with answers to all the questions.

*

Greenland sounds awfully far away from North America. But if you look at a globe, you'll see that because Greenland is so far north, it's actually quite close to the northern coast of Canada. That fact helps explain how the Norse sailors could make these journeys.

A Norse boat was only about five yards across at its widest point, and about twenty-five yards long. It had one mast that carried a huge sail, and it had oars for the times when the wind was unfavorable. A man standing on the deck would have been unprotected almost from the knees up, because the shell of the boat was very low. Imagine trying to keep your balance in heavy waves and strong winds on a boat like that! Leif Eriksson and his crew must have been happy to see land.

CELEBRATE!

Mystery of the Runes

Runes are the letters of an alphabet used by Scandinavian and other northern European peoples in the centuries before Christianity spread to their lands. The shapes of runes have lots of straight lines and angles, making them easy to carve into stone.

Runes are associated with magic and secrets, perhaps because other peoples couldn't read and understand them or maybe because only a few people in each settlement knew how to read. In fact, today some people use small stones with runes painted on them to receive messages they believe come from the spirit world.

What would your name look like spelled in runes? The illustration will show you which runes correspond to the letters in your name. With a little practice, you'll be able to write whole messages in runes if you like.

Once you know how to write in runes, you can make a "mystery" T-shirt. Use fabric paint to inscribe your name across the front of a plain T-shirt; then smile mysteriously when people ask you what it says. On the back of the shirt you can use runic writing for a secret message that only you will understand.

What about a runic T-shirt as a gift for someone else? Try writing "Dad" or "Mom" in runes; if you want, give a translation by writing the letter for each rune underneath it.

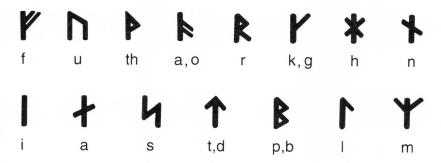

f u th a,o r k,g h n

i a s t,d p,b l m

NORSE RUNES *(you may have to substitute different letters in your name, like i for j or y)*

Tell a Heroic Tale

A Norse saga generally told the story of a hero, from his birth until his death. It often contained short sections in verse, especially if the subject of the saga was a poet. Alliteration (words beginning with the same sound) was frequently used to make the saga interesting, and clever dialogue between the characters enlivened the story.

Why not compose a saga of your own? You might want to create one about Leif Eriksson himself, using all the information you can gather about his life. But you can choose a different subject for your saga. Perhaps a member of your family has died (your grandfather or your aunt, for example) and you've heard lots of stories about that person from your mom or dad. A saga about that person can include the funny anecdotes that are part of your family lore.

A saga doesn't even have to be about a real person. You could invent a hero to star in your saga, or use a character from a book. Or you might decide to make up a saga about a cat you once owned that was a famous mouser.

A saga shouldn't sound too formal or fancy; most of the Norse sagas were told in a chatty style to listeners gathered around the fire. When you've thought up your story, practice telling it a few times; try to use some alliteration, perhaps in special phrases that you use several times ("a clever calico cat" and "hungry, heavyhearted Hank Halliday" are examples of the kind of alliteration you might use). Then record your saga on a tape. Your whole class could make a collection of sagas and play them for other classes.

October 12

Columbus Day

Christopher Columbus was not, of course, the first European to "discover" America. In fact, he wasn't looking for America; he was looking for a western route to Asia, and he believed that Asia was where he had landed. Yet Columbus is important because his reports of what he had found prompted many others to sail west from Europe; Columbus's voyages truly opened a "new world" to Europeans and changed the course of history.

What Columbus and later explorers found in the Americas was a wide range of complex and varied cultures that were thousands of years old. The meeting of European and American peoples had tragic results for Native Americans, many of whom were killed in fighting the newcomers or by European diseases they brought with them. Yet the arrival of these early immigrants was the beginning of the rich multicultural tapestry that is American society today.

October 12 is the day on which Columbus and his crew, on three small sailing ships, first reached America. Most people now believe that they landed on Samana Cay in the Bahamas. They had set out from Palos in Spain on August 3, 1492.

Columbus kept a diary, or log, of the journey from beginning to end, and this log provides a wonderfully detailed record of the journey. In it Columbus told of the things he saw day by day, and he also described his thoughts and feelings. In the log entry for October 12, 1492, the day he first landed in the Americas, Columbus wrote that he had taken possession of the island for the king and queen of Spain and named it San Salvador. He went on: "The people here called this island *Guanahani* in their language, and their speech is very fluent, although I do not understand any of it." Columbus soon began to communicate with the islanders in sign language.

Columbus's log provides a remarkable record of his journey and it gives us a picture of a fifteenth-century man whose vision of the world was different from that of most people of his time. It shows his errors and mistakes (he never did realize that he had found a previously unknown continent and he continued to believe he had come close to Japan and China) and it also shows his amazement and wonder at the new things he found. On November 27, 1492, he was on the northeastern coast of Cuba. He wrote: "Whenever I enter one of these harbors, I am detained by sheer pleasure and delight as I see and marvel at the beauty and freshness of these countries."

In recent years many people have begun to feel that traditional ways of celebrating Columbus Day don't make sense anymore. But instead of honoring Columbus as the "discoverer" of America, we can celebrate the diverse, multicultural society that we share.

Did You Know . . . ?

In his private log (a kind of diary), Columbus said that he would keep an accurate record of how many miles the ship traveled each day, but that he would write down fewer miles in the ship's official log. Why did he do this? Because he thought that his crew might become frightened as they sailed on seas that were entirely unknown; he feared they might mutiny and force him to turn back if they knew they were so far from home. In his private log, Columbus said he would record a shorter distance in the official log than the ship had actually gone in order "to sustain their hope and dispel their fears of a long voyage."

Columbus had another reason for falsifying the official log. Remember that he was looking for a westward route to the gold and jewels of Asia. If he found it, the knowledge of the route would itself be very valuable. Columbus didn't want his crew members or the captains of the ships to be able to retrace his route later on their own. To prevent them from learning the route, he wrote incorrect information in the ship's official log, keeping the true directions to himself.

*

Columbus set off on his voyage in the *Santa Maria*, the largest of the three ships. But the *Santa Maria* sank off the coast of Hispaniola (now Haiti and the Dominican Republic) and after that Columbus sailed in the *Niña*. She was a small ship called a caravel, only seventy feet long with a crew of twenty-four men. The *Niña* had two square sails and one triangular one, and she could hold fifty-one tons of cargo. As the food and drink were used up, the ship became lighter. Sometimes in bad weather this made her hard to control. So the crew filled some of the empty barrels with seawater to add weight to the ship.

*

Many people today believe the most important results of Columbus's voyages were the changes they triggered in the world's history. One amazing result was the movement across the Atlantic of many different foods. Did you know that tomatoes and corn were unknown in Europe before Columbus's time? Lots of other foods that are basic to European economies, such as potatoes in Ireland, came from America. The explorers in their turn introduced new foods to the Americas; for example, they brought oranges and lemons, which had originally come from Asia. They also brought domestic cattle and horses; as the horses spread through the continent, they transformed the way of life of many Native American cultures.

CELEBRATE!

Bridge the Communication Gap

Imagine what it was like for the Spaniards and the Native Americans when Columbus's ships first arrived. Neither group knew a single word of the other's language. They must have had to use sign language until they learned a few basic words, such as the ones for water and food. But even then it must have been impossible to talk to one another about ideas. Misunderstandings probably were pretty common.

Try a communication experiment in your class. Divide into two groups; one group acts as the explorers who come to a place they don't know, and the other pretends to be the people who live there. Each group meets and chooses a language to use. Variations on Pig Latin, such as Opp and Urb, are good possibilities (look them up in books about codes in the library). When you practice using your language with your group, make sure the other group can't hear you.

If your group is the native people, the classroom is your village. Decide who is your leader and what parts the other people play—what they do, how old they are, and anything else you feel is important.

The explorers must also choose a leader and decide where they have come from and what they expect to find. Maybe you'll have gifts or items to trade that you've brought from your home country.

When both groups are ready, start the communication experiment. Act out the events that take place, starting with the explorers' arrival. Be sure to use only your own language at all times, except for the new words the other group teaches you. This kind of improvisation is a lot of fun, but you'll probably find it's also hard work to make yourself understood without a common language.

The Best of Both Worlds

If people in the Americas had never had any contact with people on other continents, our lives would be very different. We would have only the foods that were native to North and South America. And the rest of the world wouldn't have American foods as part of their cultures. Think about Italian cooking without the tomatoes that explorers took back with them. Most European diets include a lot of potatoes, and corn as a feed for animals is important all over the world.

Try making a list of as many foods as you can that migrated from one continent to another. You may be amazed to discover that some countries' major crops didn't even exist in those places before the age of exploration.

Why not make a meal of the best of both worlds? Your feast will include only dishes that require at least one ingredient from the Americas and one from Europe, Africa, or Asia. Here are a few ideas to get you started.

	Americas	*Europe/Africa/Asia*
Main dish:	tomato sauce	spaghetti (wheat)
Salad:	pineapple slices	orange slices
Dessert:	pumpkin	pie (wheat crust)

You can make this meal at home with a friend or your family. Or you might divide your class up into teams and serve your feast as a Columbus Day celebration. Either way, the best part is eating it!

October 15

National Grouch Day

Yes, there really is a day set aside to be grouchy. It's on October 15 every year. This is the day to get up on the wrong side of the bed and scowl at anyone who dares tell you to "Have a nice day." So save up your crabby remarks and mean looks for that day. Even the sunniest personality needs a day to be plain grumpy, and this is it. But be sure to warn everyone around you what's coming!

According to the National Association of Grouches, National Grouch Day started in the late 1970s with a student who thought her teacher was the grouchiest in the world. His biggest crime was giving too much homework. Some people said that anyone chewing gum in his class had five seconds to get rid of it; otherwise that student had to wear the gum on his nose for the rest of the day. It seems the teacher really hated it when students passed notes in his class—he read any notes he intercepted over the school PA system. So one of his students got the idea of starting a new holiday—National Grouch Day—that would be celebrated on the teacher's birthday.

While National Grouch Day is a fairly new idea, being grumpy and crabby is probably as old as humankind. Think of all the mean and grouchy people you've read about, like the witches in *The Wizard of Oz* and "Hansel and Gretel." Remember Grumpy in the Disney movie of *Snow White*? And you probably know some people yourself who always seem to complain and be in a bad temper.

Wouldn't it be great if the grouches you know could get all that crabbiness and grumpiness out of their systems on National Grouch Day and have a good time the rest of the year? You could try suggesting this idea, but be sure to catch the grouch you know on one of his or her less grouchy days!

Did You Know . . . ?

The student who started National Grouch Day was Monica Moeller. Her teacher's name was Alan R. Miller and the school was Carter Middle School in Clio, Michigan. Do you know anyone who goes to school there?

*

You can get your own Grouch License from the National Association of Grouches. (The group's initials are N.A.G.) Here's what the license says: "This license gives you full permission to be a stinkin' lousy grouch. BIG DEAL! So you've got your license—leave me alone, STUPID! I've got work to do!"

Send your request to the National Association of Grouches, 12281 Alexander Street, Clio, MI 48420. If you're generally a cheerful person and not always a grouch, it would be nice to include a self-addressed, stamped envelope with your request. This license allows you to be a total grouch only on October 15.

CELEBRATE!

Hold a Grouch Day Grump-Out

Why not hold your own National Grouch Day festivities? If this holiday falls on a school day, you could involve the whole class. Or, if October 15 is on the weekend, you might want to have a party at your house. You could serve grumpy burgers with mean sauce and have pickle-juice cola to drink. But remember that you won't get any help in the kitchen because Mom and Dad have a right to be grouchy that day too.

Make a banner

Use a roll of inexpensive shelf paper to make a big banner for Grouch Day. With poster paint or marking pens, write "National Grouch Day—October 15" in giant letters across the middle. Then get all your friends and family members to write "I get grouchy when . . ." lists on separate pieces of paper. Pin or tape the grouch lists along the bottom of the banner and put up the banner where everyone can read the lists.

You'll all get a lot of laughs reading what makes people grouchy, but you might also be surprised at the things you find out. Sitting down to make your own list makes you think about the things that really bother you. If hearing your alarm shrill at you in the morning makes you crabby all day at school, maybe you'll decide to save your money to buy a clock radio and wake up to cheerful music instead. And if your friend discovers that his habit of calling you every night to get the math assignment he forgot to bring home really drives you crazy, perhaps he can get organized and remember those assignments from now on.

Hold a contest

You'll probably want to hold a "worst grouch ever" contest on National Grouch Day. Make sure that there's a ballot box and that all the nominations are secret. Have everyone write down some reasons for their choices when they fill in their ballots. Read out the votes in the middle of the festivities so that your king or queen of the grouches can enjoy reigning for the rest of the day.

Of course Grouch Day celebrations are all in fun and

shouldn't be mean. But this is a good opportunity to find out how you and others feel. Will you be surprised if you get lots of votes as the biggest grouch ever?

Send grouchy greetings

There aren't any greeting cards in the stores for National Grouch Day, but you can have fun making your own. Think up whatever is the opposite of most greeting card sayings— "Have a miserable birthday" or "Glad to hear you're sick" are just the beginning. And be sure to tell all your friends to have a rotten day or bad luck on the test when you see them at school.

*

Remember that Grouch Day comes only once a year. So get all your grouchiness over with on October 15. The next day it won't be funny anymore.

October 16

Dictionary Day

Dictionary Day celebrates the birthday of Noah Webster, who wrote the first American dictionary. He worked on a short one first, which was published in 1806, only twenty-three years after the end of the Revolutionary War.

Then he spent twenty-two years writing a huge dictionary for Americans. Called *The American Dictionary of the English Language*, it defined seventy thousand words. Twelve thousand of them were new words that Americans used—words like *skunk*, *bullfrog*, *squash*, and *banjo*. The last word in this dictionary was *zygomatic* (you'll have to look up its meaning).

Webster's name has been associated with dictionaries ever since. And in 1961 *Webster's Third New International Dictionary of the English Language, Unabridged* was published. It defines more than 450,000 words and is 2,662 pages long. The last word in this dictionary is *zyzzogeton* (you'll enjoy looking up this one, too).

Many of the new words in this dictionary came from scientific discoveries and from changes in the life-style of the American people. There hadn't been a need for the words *smog* and *astronaut* in earlier times. And Webster himself wouldn't have known what an *automobile* was, because he died long before cars were invented.

Dictionaries are everywhere—libraries, schools, homes, bookstores, even at the supermarket checkout counter. Just about everybody uses one from time to time, to check a word's spelling or pronunciation or to find out exactly what a word means. They're quick and easy to use, but deciding which new words to add and how to define them is hard work!

Did You Know . . . ?

The Oxford English Dictionary (OED) is the biggest dictionary in the English language. In 1928 the first edition of the OED was published. It had ten volumes and took seventy-one years to write. The second edition, published in 1989, has twenty volumes, more than twenty thousand pages, and costs $2500. There's also a condensed version that comes in two volumes; the print is so small that a magnifying glass comes with the dictionary!

*

The shortest words are one letter long—*a*, *I*, even *o*. But what's the longest? *Antidisestablishmentarianism* used to be the longest English word, with twenty-eight letters, but later the name of a lung disease won the prize—*pneumono-ultramicroscopicsilicovolcanoconiosis* has forty-five letters! Very few people know what these words mean, and even fewer people use them in conversation. To keep track of which English word is the longest, check the *Guinness Book of Records* every year under the topic "Words, longest."

*

Webster's and the OED aren't the only dictionaries of the English language—lots of other good ones are available, such as the *New American Heritage Dictionary*. On the library reference shelves you'll also find all kinds of specialized dictionaries—medical, legal, mathematical, even computer terms. Of course there are dictionaries in two languages: maybe you've used one that tells what a French or Spanish word means in English. But did you know that there are dictionaries of rhyming words especially for song writers and poets? And you might enjoy paging through a dictionary of slang.

CELEBRATE!

Sling Some Slang

People like to use words in new ways, and they like to use up-to-date slang. You've probably noticed that a word suddenly catches on in your school and pretty soon everybody's using it. But outsiders may not know what the new word means. Help them out—make your own slang dictionary.

Here's how. You need a small looseleaf binder or a pack of index cards. These make it easy to keep the words in alphabetical order as you add them. Use a new page or card for each word. If it's a word someone made up, think about the best way to spell it. Put alternate spellings, if there are any, in parentheses after the word. A pronunciation guide may be helpful for some words.

On the next line write in the definition. It's often hard to define a word exactly and clearly, so make some notes before you write it down in ink. Consult your friends. They may have other definitions or they may come up with synonyms that help define the word. An easy way to help people understand a new word is to use it in a sentence; adding one or two to your definition might be a good idea.

Put a date on each word you add to your slang dictionary. You'll be amazed at how quickly some words go out of style. And be sure to have extra pages or index cards handy so you can add the latest slang word when it appears.

> **dudical**
> based on the word *dude*; means in the manner of a dude (someone who's cool, a person who really knows what's happening); also means "excellent" or "terrific."
> *Example*: He made some dudical comment that made the whole class laugh.

"The Definition, Please"

You need at least three or four people to play this game. Each player looks up three (or more) words in a dictionary and copies down a brief definition for each. Take turns reading one of your words to the other players. They say what they think it means and the person whose definition is closest to the real one gets a point. If no one can define the word, you get a point. After all the words have been used, count up the points to see who wins.

Try playing this game with your family as well as with your friends. You might be surprised at how much you know and at how much you can guess about words you've never even heard before.

*

As you'll see, two holidays in this book fall on October 16— Dictionary Day and World Food Day. They have entirely different purposes and meanings, and both have terrific projects for you and your friends to try. So why not celebrate two holidays on one day? Maybe you'll come up with a way of celebrating that's perfect for both holidays together.

October 16

World Food Day

The first World Food Day was held in 1981. The date of the holiday, October 16, is the anniversary of the founding of the United Nations Food and Agriculture Organization (FAO) in 1945. The concept of the holiday is clear from its name—it is one day set aside during the year for people around the world to think about the hunger that still exists and to try to do something for those who don't have enough to eat.

You may not know anyone who really doesn't have any way of getting enough food to stay alive. But there are millions of people in countries all over the world, including the United States, who face malnutrition and starvation every day. During this decade 100 million children will die from preventable malnutrition and from diseases that it causes. The young and the elderly are especially vulnerable to the problems that come from malnutrition, but everyone needs food to survive.

Homelessness is an increasing problem in the United States and in many other nations. With homelessness usually comes hunger. But even people who have homes often go hungry. Imagine never knowing whether you were going to get a meal. What would it be like to see your parents giving up the only food they had so that you could eat? How would it feel to go to school with no breakfast and not have the money to get lunch? What if you didn't think you'd get dinner that night either? It's hard to believe that kids just like you go hungry day after day, but they do. So do adults.

The purpose of World Food Day is to increase everyone's awareness of the global problem of hunger. It is observed in 150 nations and has the support of more than four hundred organizations in the United States. This day is the focal point of work that goes on all year in many government agencies and private organizations. It's a day for you to start thinking about this worldwide problem and to take a step to help.

Did You Know . . . ?

Even during World War II, nations from all over the world were concerned that the people of some countries didn't have enough to eat. Representatives of forty-four nations met in Virginia in 1943 to start a worldwide agricultural group that would "assure each country the food it needs." Eventually this became the UN Food and Agriculture Organization. Its motto is *Fiat Panis*, which in Latin means "Let there be bread."

*

Did you know that the United States is the world's largest exporter *and* importer of food? Nearly half of the world's grain reserves are in the U.S. and Canada, and these two countries provide almost two-thirds of all food aid. Yet thousands of children and adults go hungry in these two countries every day.

*

There is a National Committee for World Food Day at 1001 22nd Street N.W., Washington, DC 20437. This office has lots of literature and materials available, some of it especially designed for schools to use. You can write to this committee and ask for information on how to start a World Food Day program in your school.

Another organization, Oxfam America, encourages people in the United States to fast on the Thursday before Thanksgiving. Those who participate in the fast send the cost of the meal they didn't eat to Oxfam America to support their work. If you want to know more about this idea, write to Fast for a World Harvest, 115 Broadway, Boston, MA 02116. Or call their toll-free number: 1-800-597-FAST.

CELEBRATE!

Banking on Food

The first purpose of World Food Day is to make people aware of the problem. But next comes action. You and your friends can become part of the solution. Almost every community has a food bank—a community or religious center that stores canned and dry food and gives it to people who need it.

You can volunteer to help at the food bank. Maybe you could work with the people who sort out and put away food that is donated. Or perhaps you can deliver flyers for their food drives or bicycle around and post them on community bulletin boards.

Start your own food drive

A great project for you and your friends or your class is to hold your own drive for the food bank in your community. Why not have it the week before World Food Day? That way you can collect canned and dry food for people who need it and at the same time remind everyone who sees your banners that World Food Day is coming—a day to think about the problems of hunger all over the world.

Get the info first

Contact the food bank and find out what sorts of things they will accept. It's important to observe health and safety rules when accepting food donations and storing food for any period of time. See if you can get a few parents to help out by transporting the food you collect to the food bank. Also, you'll need some clean cardboard cartons to hold this food.

Get groups to help

It's often a good idea to hold your food drive in collaboration with your school or a religious organization. If you decide to do this, be sure to check with the principal of the school or the people in charge to find out where you can put up your stand. You'll want at least one big banner saying something like "World Food Day—October 16: Help Stamp Out Hunger!"

Borrow a long table for people to put their food donations on and hang another banner along the front of it like a skirt. Then you can put the cartons under the table ready to fill up. Be sure to let people know what days and hours they can make donations, and organize a group of volunteers to stand behind the table and answer questions.

Advertise

Make up leaflets to copy and post on all available bulletin boards. List exactly what foods are most needed and let people know the rules—are foods in jars okay and is it better to give two small cans or one large one? This is a good time for parents to clean out their shelves of that special kind of canned fruit that you loved until last month or those packages of flavored noodles your mom bought before she went on her latest diet.

A different way to do it

Another place you might be able to set up your food-collection stand is in front of the local supermarket (ask the manager if this is okay). This would be a good location for your scout troop to get donations for the food bank. You'll need someone who drives to come at the end of each day and pick up what's been collected; maybe the store manager will let you leave your table and banners inside the store for the night. You may find that he or she is happy to help with your project, because it means a little more business for the store and it makes customers feel good about shopping there.

It's easy to get people who are going into the market to buy one or two extra cans or boxes of food and set them on your table as they leave. Be sure to make a banner listing the foods you want most in big letters.

*

A successful food drive means a lot of work in packing everything up and hauling it to the food bank. But the more you collect, the more meals you'll be providing to people who would otherwise go hungry.

Let the World Know

You can spread the word about World Food Day to other countries. After all, it's an international problem; adults and kids everywhere need to work together to solve it.

Linking to let people know

Why not start a letter or postcard chain to get people thinking about World Food Day? Sometimes these chains go around the world and reach the most amazing people. Send your cards to four friends or relatives in different parts of the country, and then see what happens. Your postcard could say something as simple as "World Food Day, October 16. Do one thing today to help stop hunger. Send out four postcards like this to people you know and we can change the world!"

Hands across the sea

Do you have a pen pal who lives overseas? Encourage him or her to organize a World Food Day food drive in that community. Explain how you've done this in your school or scout troop; this will help your pen pal see that it's not so difficult to do.

If you would like to become a pen pal, there are a number

of groups you can write to. They will try to match you with someone who is about your age. Here are a few:

International Pen Friends
PO Box 2409
Monroe, MI 48161

Student Letter Exchange
910 Fourth Street SE
Austin, MN 55912

League of Friendship, Inc.
PO Box 509
Mount Vernon, OH 43050

World Pen Pals
1690 Como Avenue
St. Paul, MN 55108

October 24

United Nations Day

United Nations Day has been celebrated since 1948, when it was created to commemorate the beginning of the United Nations on October 24, 1945. When the United Nations began, it had fifty-one member countries. Since then more than one hundred other countries have joined this organization.

The main goals of the United Nations are to maintain international peace, to promote equal rights and peoples' self-determination, and to achieve cooperative solutions to international economic, social, cultural, and humanitarian problems. The UN helps countries resolve disputes and deals with everything of general concern to humanity. In addition to working for international peace, the UN is concerned with such topics as the environment, outer space, the oceans, drug control, and global hunger.

There are six main parts of the UN: the General Assembly, the Security Council, the Economic and Social Council, the Trusteeship Council, the Secretariat, and the International Court of Justice (also known as the World Court). Each member country of the UN, whether small or large, rich or poor, has one vote in the General Assembly. The Assembly meets from mid-September to mid-December every year at the UN headquarters in New York City. Members discuss important questions and set UN policy on these issues.

The Security Council, whose function is peacekeeping in the world, has fifteen members. Five of these were established as permanent members—China, France, the Soviet Union (now represented by Russia), the United Kingdom, and the United States. The other ten places on the Council rotate among the other members of the UN. All important decisions require nine "yes" votes, including those of all five permanent members.

The Economic and Social Council is responsible for carrying out the policies set by the UN General Assembly to promote prosperity in developing countries, guarantee human rights, and promote the other goals of the UN. The Trusteeship Council was originally created to oversee the movement toward independence of non-self-governing areas of the world (Trust Territories). Largely through its efforts, almost all of the Trust Territories have now achieved independence. Representatives from various countries take turns as members of these two Councils as well as the International Court.

The Secretariat of the UN is the part that makes the whole organization run smoothly. The UN has more than twenty thousand employees around the world, working as translators, lawyers, experts in various fields, tour guides, security officers, clerks, and so on.

The idea behind the United Nations is that when world leaders meet and talk over their problems and differences, useful and peaceful solutions can be found. Representatives from member nations have a chance to bring up all sorts of difficulties their countries are facing. Others may have suggestions and ideas that will help. This kind of give-and-take and group concern aids everyone.

Although the United Nations General Assembly cannot pass laws that other nations have to obey, its decisions and recommendations carry the weight of world opinion. Advice and suggestions from this group are not easy to ignore. And while the United Nations is not a world government, it is the best hope we now have for attaining global peace, justice, and freedom.

Did You Know . . . ?

The United Nations Economic and Social Council has fifty-four members and splits its meetings between New York City and Geneva, Switzerland. The International Court of Justice is located in The Hague, Netherlands.

*

The Headquarters of the UN was built on an eighteen-acre piece of land next to the East River in New York City. Much of this land was donated by John D. Rockefeller, Jr. The rest was given by the city of New York. There are parklike grounds and four buildings: the General Assembly building, a thirty-nine-story Secretariat tower, a conference building near the river, and the Dag Hammarskjöld Library. (Dag Hammarskjöld was the Secretary-General of the UN from 1953 until his death in a plane crash in 1961.)

*

There are six official languages used at the UN—Arabic, Chinese, English, French, Russian, and Spanish. Every seat in the Assembly has earphones so that representatives can hear simultaneous translations in these languages of what the speaker is saying. Most signs at UN Headquarters are in English and French.

*

If you visit New York City, you can take a guided tour of the UN. If a meeting is going on while you're there, you may be able to go and watch it. You can also write to the UN for information about any part of its activities: Public Inquiries Unit, United Nations, New York, NY 10017.

CELEBRATE!

Tracing Your Roots

The United States is often called the "melting pot" because its people came from all over the world. You might have a friend who was born in another country and you're likely to know someone whose parents or grandparents were born somewhere else. But even people whose grandparents and great-grandparents and great-great-grandparents were born in the United States probably can trace their ancestry to another country. In fact, the only people in the whole country whose ancestors didn't come from another land in the last five centuries are Native Americans.

What's your heritage?

Do you know where your family came from? Many people are interested in tracing their roots. A good way to start is to talk to your parents and other older relatives; they're likely to have lots of information. You might discover that your mom's family came originally from England, while your dad's people came from Russia. Perhaps your ancestors are a mixture of people from Africa and South America. Or some of your grandparents may have come from a Scandinavian country while others came from somewhere in Asia. You might have ancestors from half a dozen countries or from only one.

Picture your world

It's interesting to find out your own family's roots and to share them with your friends. If you colored in on a map all the countries you and your friends represent, how much of the world would you cover?

Hold a Heritage Party

A fun way to celebrate United Nations Day is to hold a Heritage Party. Each person needs to choose a nationality—either the country where one of your ancestors was born or a place that you find particularly fascinating.

Dress your part

Put together a costume to represent the country you have chosen. It doesn't need to be a whole outfit; a few props will do fine. For instance, a shamrock cut out of green paper and pinned to your shirt will probably let everyone know you're from Ireland. But many countries don't have an easily recognized symbol or article of clothing, so you may have to be pretty inventive.

If you have a few jokey prizes, you can award them to the people who guess the largest number of countries correctly based on the costumes.

International food and music

Of course, the best part of a party like this one is the food. A relative who specializes in a terrific national dish will probably be happy to cook up a batch for you and your friends. Or you can make your own ethnic dishes by following recipes in a cookbook from the library.

For the musical background of your party, each person can make a short tape of ethnic songs from the radio or records or even family sing-alongs. And if anyone knows a dance or song from his or her country of origin, this is the perfect time for the whole group of you to learn it.

Trace Your Roots Through Stamps

United Nations Day is a good day to share your international stamp collection or to start one. Stamp collecting is a hobby that has turned into a profitable business for many people.

And it's fun to see how the looks of a country's stamps change as the politics of that country shift over the years.

You may want to specialize in stamps of one particular country or collect them from all over the world. Friends who travel a lot are usually happy to send you postcards from wherever they go. Perhaps they can also buy an assortment of new stamps at a foreign post office to bring home to you. Contact your own local post office or check stamp-collecting magazines in the library for the location of the nearest philatelic society or group to get you started.

October 31

Halloween

For kids in the United States, Halloween means trick-or-treating and wearing scary costumes and having a lot of fun. But how did it get started? In ancient times the Celts, who lived in what are now England, Ireland, and northern France, celebrated the festival of Samhain (pronounced "Sah-wen") at this time of year. It was the night before their new year began, and it marked the end of the harvest season and the beginning of winter's cold. The Celts believed that on this night witches and ghosts roamed around and that the souls of dead people came back to visit the places where they had lived. Huge bonfires were lit to scare away the witches, while food and lanterns were put out to make the dead souls feel at home.

Later, Roman conquerors combined their own festival to honor the dead with the celebration of Samhain. When the Catholic Church decided in the 800s to make November 1 a holy day called All Saints or All Hallows Day, the evening of the day before became All Hallows Even or Eve. (The "v" eventually got dropped and the name became Halloween.) Though the Church tried to discourage the old ideas, people still clung to the belief that dead souls were in the air on that night. That's probably why ghosts are part of the lore of Halloween today.

Even as Christianity became more widespread, some of the old pagan beliefs and customs lingered on. In Ireland especially, people thought that ghosts and spirits roamed after dark on Halloween. They lit candles or lanterns to keep the spirits away, and if they had to go outside, they wore costumes and masks to frighten the spirits or to keep from being recognized by these unearthly beings.

The Irish were also the inventors of the trick-or-treat idea. Centuries ago groups of villagers in Ireland went from house to house on Halloween to beg for food for a community feast. (No one wanted to be alone on this scary night.) Those who gave generously were promised a prosperous year, while those who were stingy were threatened with all kinds of troubles. It wasn't until many Irish people came to the United States in the 1800s that Halloween became really popular here. In fact, Ireland is the only place where Halloween is a national holiday.

The phrase "Trick or treat!" means, of course, "Give me a treat or I'll play a trick on you." Your grandparents may remember their own Halloween pranks, such as drawing on people's windows with soap or greasing the doorknob of someone's house so it would be impossible to turn. Even today some kids play tricks, but usually they are happy to take a treat and not trick anyone.

In recent years, many children have gone trick-or-treating for UNICEF (the United Nations Children's Fund). This agency of the United Nations raises money to help children all over the world, especially where there is great need. Boxes are passed out in schools and children ask for coins for UNICEF along with treats for themselves.

Sadly, in recent years some people have played truly evil tricks on little kids who come to their houses. So parents now tell children not to eat their treats until they look them over carefully, and they make sure kids don't go trick-or-treating by themselves. In spite of this, Halloween is still fun. It's the one night of the year when you can step out of your ordinary self and become a ghoulish monster. It's a time when it's fun to scare and be scared along with all your friends.

Did You Know . . . ?

Harry Houdini was the most famous magician and escape artist of his day, and his name has come to mean a person who can get out of seemingly escape-proof traps and locked containers. He died on Halloween in 1926, and the anniversary of his death is observed by many groups of magicians. In fact, October 31 is also National Magic Day, which fits right in with the whole spirit of Halloween.

*

Jack-o'-lanterns, the carved pumpkins that symbolize Halloween, have a very long history. Old Irish legends tell of a man called Jack who tricked the devil. As a punishment, the devil made him walk through the world forever. Some versions of the story say that the devil gave Jack a burning coal and Jack put it inside the turnip he was eating, to make a lantern to light his way. Placing a candle inside a hollowed and carved turnip became a popular Halloween custom and people still do this today in Ireland and other parts of Europe. But turnips aren't so easy to carve. People in the United States found it much simpler to use large pumpkins for their jack-o'-lanterns.

*

In Singapore and other parts of Asia, according to Taoist tradition, the seventh lunar month (in late summer) is the "month of the hungry ghosts." Taoism is an ancient religion; its believers try to follow the *tao* (the way) that creates harmony in the world. The ghosts are spirits of the dead who come out to search for food and who often create mischief during this month. Sounds a lot like Halloween, doesn't it?

CELEBRATE!

Tell a Ghostly Tale

Just like the Irish of centuries ago, most people today don't want to be alone on Halloween. Here's a great way for you and some friends to scare yourselves silly as you look over your treats. Turn the lights down low and tell some ghastly ghost stories.

The most inventive way of telling ghost stories is for one person to start the story and each of the others to take a turn adding to it. Think up a good beginning for a story, using a traditional Halloween-type situation. Try one of these:

> It was a dark and stormy night and I had many miles to travel on the lonely road. . . .

> I was sitting in the house alone, wondering where everyone had gone. Suddenly the lights went out. In the eerie silence, I heard the basement door creak open. . . .

> As the fog swirled around me, I saw that the grave was open. Horror-struck, I watched the lid of the coffin begin to rise. . . .

Include as many scary words in your story as possible. Some good ones are spooky, gruesome, eerie, weird, frightful, graveyard, tombstone, coffin, skeleton, skull, bat, goblin, monster, phantom, ghost, moan, groan, shiver, tremble, haunt, creak.

Sound effects will make your ghost story even scarier. Of course, if the wind is howling around your house and branches are tapping at the window, use these sounds in your gory tale. But you can also provide props for each story-teller to use whenever appropriate. A sheet of aluminum foil can be rattled to sound like thunder; crackly cellophane or candy wrappers can be crinkled in your hand to sound like a fire. A chain is great for ghosts from the dungeon, and blowing across the top of a soda bottle makes an eerie moan.

Whether each person tells a whole story or you all add to a group story, you'll be shivering in your boots by the time it's done.

How to Haunt Houses

A "haunted house" makes a terrific addition to any Halloween party. You can put one together for your own party, or you and a couple of friends can produce one for a party for younger children.

You need a room that can be closed off from the rest of the party and very dimly lit. You'll be escorting the partygoers one at a time through "Dracula's Castle" or "Bluebeard's Tower" or whatever horrible name you come up with. Each person will be blindfolded and you'll explain what dreadful items are in the room while the blindfolded person touches each one.

You get to use your imagination at its weirdest in creating the chamber of horrors. For instance, a small bowl of peeled grapes can be a collection of eyeballs; a dish of cold cooked spaghetti is the dead man's guts. Cut-up pieces of wet sponge make great brains and dried kernels of corn or unpopped popcorn make perfect teeth. A rubber glove stuffed with wet paper towels becomes a dead hand; keep it in a shallow dish of water so it feels clammy on the outside when it's touched. Put a ring on one of its fingers for a more gruesome effect.

Be sure to hang strands of black thread in the doorway for a spiderweb that brushes against the victims' faces as they enter. And if you can make a tape of eerie moans and screeches to play in the background, it adds a lot to the scary atmosphere.

As the guide to the horror chamber, you can wear all-black clothes and rubber gloves; tell your victims while you tie their blindfolds that you've just come from helping your master cut up a body. Speak softly as you describe the awful items; your gentle manner as you guide the blindfolded victims makes things even creepier. (*Warning*: Some little kids may get truly terrified. If they do, don't force them to keep going; just take off their blindfolds and show them what the things really are. But ask them not to tell anyone else and spoil the fun.)

November 3

National Sandwich Day

What's a sandwich? Two slices of bread with something in between them, right? A sandwich is such a handy thing to eat (it's easy to hold and carry with you from place to place; the bread helps keep your hands from getting messy; it tastes good) that it seems as if people must have known about it forever. But they haven't.

Supposedly, sandwiches were invented by an Englishman named John Montagu, Fourth Earl of Sandwich, who was born on November 3, 1718. He liked to gamble, and the legend says that one day when he was feeling lucky, he didn't want to leave the gambling table to eat. The earl told his servant to bring him some meat between two slices of bread, so he could eat quickly and easily while still playing cards. Other people thought this was a terrific idea, and they called this new style of food a "sandwich" after its inventor.

Sandwiches come in all shapes and sizes, from fancy tea sandwiches cut in neat triangles with all the crusts trimmed off to six-foot overstuffed hero sandwiches that can feed a crowd. People make sandwiches on croissants, bagels, pita bread, and hard rolls as well as regular bread, and they fill them with just about anything that's edible. Combinations like peanut butter and dill pickles or baked beans and lettuce used to be considered a little weird, but now they're just an ordinary lunch for lots of people.

When is a sandwich not a sandwich? If you start thinking about it, there are lots of variations on the basic idea of a sandwich. Try making a list of all the different kinds you can think of. For instance, do s'mores (graham crackers with chocolate and toasted marshmallow in between) count as sandwiches? And what about tacos, or croissants that are baked with filling already inside, or ice cream sandwiches? Once you get started, you'll be amazed at all the different possibilities you come up with.

What's your favorite sandwich? Whether it's a tried-and-true peanut-butter-and-jelly or something unusual like a spaghetti sandwich or one filled with raw carrots and celery, National Sandwich Day is the perfect time to eat it.

Did You Know . . . ?

Did you ever hear of a "Dagwood sandwich"? In a comic strip called *Blondie* that has been popular since the 1930s, Blondie's husband Dagwood loves to make himself a sandwich for his midnight snack. But Dagwood's sandwich is never just two pieces of bread and a little something in between. It's a wobbling tower of everything Dagwood can find in the refrigerator—sliced meat, lettuce, tomatoes, hard-boiled eggs, pickles, olives, sardines, cheese, baked beans, onion, and of course ketchup—all stacked precariously between a top and a bottom slice of bread. Dagwood often has problems keeping the top slice of bread balanced on top of his sky-scraper sandwich. But the idea sounds kind of tasty, doesn't it?

*

Did you ever hear of the Sandwich Islands? That was the name Captain Cook gave to the islands we now call Hawaii when he came upon them in 1778. He named them after the same Earl of Sandwich who invented sandwiches, because at that time the earl was the First Lord of the Admiralty in England, and that meant he was Captain Cook's boss.

There is a town in England called Sandwich. Wonder what they eat for lunch there. There are also Sandwiches in Illinois and Massachusetts.

*

National Sandwich Day was started by the company that makes Ziploc® sandwich bags. They have a contest every year for the best sandwich recipes sent in by students all over the U.S. If you'd like to enter your favorite sandwich in the contest, write for information to: ZIPLOC® National Sandwich Contest, DowBrands Food Care Division, PO Box 78980, New Augusta, IN 46278.

CELEBRATE!

Sandwich Grab Bag

If you're like most kids, you take a sandwich to school for your lunch almost every day. But sometimes, even if you make your lunch yourself, you get bored with the same old stuff day in and day out. Here's a great way to celebrate National Sandwich Day with your whole class and have something new and different for lunch.

Ask each person in your class to bring a sandwich to school on November 3. When you're making your sandwich, use your creativity to make it the best sandwich you can think of—one you'd love to eat anytime. Each class member should put his or her sandwich in a brown paper lunch bag (or any kind of bag you can't see through).

At school, put all the sandwiches in a box or basket and then draw numbers out of a hat to see who gets to pick a sandwich first, then second, and so on. When everyone has drawn a sandwich, open them up and start eating. You might be surprised at the interesting new ideas your friends have come up with, and maybe you'll be inspired to make some different lunches for yourself.

An even better grab bag

To make your grab bag event even more exciting, here's a different twist. Start out the same way: Person #1 draws a sandwich out of the box and opens it so everyone can see what kind it is. Then Person #2 draws a sandwich and opens it; if #2 likes #1's sandwich better, he or she can make Person #1 trade sandwiches. But wait—no one gets to start eating until everyone has drawn a sandwich. And the later numbers can force a trade with anyone who has already gotten a sandwich. So Person #3 can trade with either #1 or #2; Person #4 can trade with #1, #2, or #3; and so on. You can see it's lucky to have a high number for this version of the Sandwich Grab Bag!

You could make this event into your own Sandwich Contest in class. Take a vote on which sandwich was the healthiest, or the most unusual, or the messiest to eat, or just the most delicious.

Note: To make the Sandwich Grab Bag totally successful, it's a good idea to find out in advance if anyone in your class is allergic to certain foods or has other dietary restrictions. For example, some people in your class may be vegetarians, or they may keep kosher. Find out exactly what restrictions apply. Then make sure all the sandwiches can be eaten by everyone, or mark the wrappers of the ones certain people can't eat so they'll be sure not to pick those. After all, if you're allergic to sardines, it won't be much fun if you draw a sardine-and-tomato sandwich!

Sweet Sandwiches?

But wait! Lunch isn't over yet. What about dessert? Even if the Earl of Sandwich didn't think of dessert sandwiches, there's no reason why you can't. Since desserts are usually sweet, you'll want to come up with an outside and inside that go together in a sweet taste treat. Of course, there are ice cream sandwiches with cookies or slices of cake as the "bread" and ice cream as the filling. But can't you think up something more exotic?

What about a fruit-and-cake sandwich? Sliced peaches between thin squares of cake would be delicious. Or maybe you'd prefer slices of banana sandwiched between halves of a sweet biscuit that's been spread with strawberry jam. You could make your own version of a sandwich cookie by spreading the bottoms of two chocolate chip cookies with peanut butter and sticking them together.

Almost anything that's got two outside layers with a filling between them will qualify as a sandwich, so let your imagination run wild. Why not stick together two slices of watermelon spread with cream cheese? How does a sandwich made of two round slices of whole orange and a slab of chocolate ice cream in the middle sound to you (besides messy)?

The perfect way to top off your Sandwich Day grab bag is to hold a Dessert Sandwich Fest afterward. Bring your best creations and put them all on a tray so the whole crowd can judge which looks the best before you all dig in.

Happy Sandwich Day!

November 11

Veterans Day

Originally called Armistice Day, Veterans Day commemorates the ending of World War I on November 11, 1918. This war, which was also called the Great War, had one of the highest casualty rates in history. On one side were the Allies (chiefly France, Britain, Russia, and the United States) and on the other were the Central or Axis Powers (Germany, Austria-Hungary, and Turkey). Out of a total of 65 million men who served in the armies of both sides, 10 million were killed and twice that number were injured.

When the armistice, or truce, was signed on November 11 and the soldiers laid down their weapons and began coming home, the whole world sighed with relief. Everyone hoped there would never be such a terrible and bloody war again. People wanted to remember the ending of that horrible conflict and began celebrating Armistice Day to remind themselves of the price we all pay for war and of their hopes that there would never be another.

Of course there was another world war, and another peace settlement. By the 1950s Armistice Day had taken on another significance. It was a day not only to honor those who had lost their lives in World War I but to honor all those who have served in the Armed Forces of the United States. In 1954 the name of Armistice Day was officially changed to Veterans Day. However, in some places Veterans Day is still called Armistice Day, and in others it's called Remembrance Day, Victory Day, or World War I Memorial Day.

Through 1970 Veterans Day was celebrated on November 11, the actual date of the armistice ending World War I. Then, in 1971, a law was passed to make Veterans Day fall on the fourth Monday in October. The idea was that this would give everyone another three-day holiday weekend in the year. But many people felt that the significance of a day to honor those who fought for our country was lost when it became a movable holiday. One after another, various states began celebrating Veterans Day on November 11 again. Finally the law was changed, and in 1978 the official observance of Veterans Day once again became November 11.

Did You Know . . . ?

When the armistice agreement to end World War I was signed on November 11, 1918, it said that the fighting would stop at 11:00 A.M. that day. That meant that the soldiers laid down their weapons at the eleventh hour of the eleventh day of the eleventh month. In many places in the United States people observe a silent memorial at the eleventh hour of the eleventh day of the eleventh month every year.

*

Have you noticed artificial red poppies in people's buttonholes on Veterans Day? Do you wonder where they come from and why? Those poppies are the traditional thank-you gift to people who donate to the Disabled American Veterans organization. The idea of using red poppies came, at least in part, from a poem written during World War I. "In Flanders Fields" was written by a Canadian serviceman named John McCrae while he was serving in the army. It talks about the courage of soldiers and tells of the huge battlefield cemetery in the part of Europe called Flanders where thousands of red poppies grow among the grave markers. Sadly, Mr. McCrae was killed in action in 1918, but his poem was published in a British magazine called *Punch* on December 8, 1919, and was famous for many years after.

CELEBRATE!

A Basket of Fun

What could be better than an event where you get to help others and have a good time yourself? This is a great project to do with a couple of friends, with your whole class, or with your scout troop or other club. Each person needs a collection of favorite board games and books, packed up in a shopping bag or backpack.

Nearly every large town and city has a VA (Veterans Administration) hospital or similar facility. Look in the phone book for one near you or call the local number for the Veterans Administration. Ask the activities director if your group can come and visit on Veterans Day to spend time with some of the veterans. Explain that you want to bring games to play and books to read. If you have computer games you're good at, ask if they have computer equipment to play them on. (You won't be leaving these things at the hospital, just taking them to use while you're there.)

Many of the patients at these facilities have been there a long time and probably don't have a lot of visitors. They will really appreciate having someone new to talk to and do things with. Don't be surprised if you find a Monopoly fanatic or someone who's a whiz at Clue. You might even come across someone who can help you make the model you're constructing look just like the real thing!

A Veterans Day Tribute

Do you or any of your friends have a relative who served in the United States Armed Forces? Most kids do, because millions of men and women have served our country, both in peacetime and in war. One traditional way of honoring those people is to visit a military cemetery on Veterans Day.

It's not necessary to know or be related to anyone who is buried there. After all, those men and women didn't know you either but they were still willing to fight for the country we live in and for the freedoms our country represents.

If there are still flowers blooming in your house or garden, ask if you can pick a few to take with you. If not, see if there are some small branches of evergreen bush or tree that you can cut and take. Try to take something that was grown (not artificial flowers) so that when it dries up and blows away, it can become part of the soil again instead of adding to our environmental problems.

As you walk past the grave markers, you and your friends can decide where you want to lay your flowers or evergreen. Maybe you'll choose the grave of a woman who had the same first name as your aunt or perhaps you'll pick someone who died the year you were born. Whatever you decide, you'll be honoring not only that person but all the others who defended our country in peace and war.

November, fourth Thursday

Thanksgiving

The first American Thanksgiving was celebrated in 1621, the year after the Pilgrims landed at Plymouth Rock. Throughout the centuries people in many other lands have had celebrations to give thanks for a bountiful harvest. But the first Thanksgiving in North America was especially important to the new settlers and to American history. Without that good fall harvest and the advice and help of Native Americans who told them which crops would do well, the Pilgrims would not have survived.

About fifty Pilgrims and about ninety Native Americans were at the first Thanksgiving feast. Wild turkeys, which were found only in North America, were the main course. And ever since then turkey has been the traditional Thanksgiving food. Probably pumpkins or squash and cranberries, foods native to North America, were on the menu also. Cranberries grew wild in the New England bogs, and the Native Americans had showed the Pilgrims how to grow and cook corn and pumpkins.

The first presidential holiday proclamation ever made was by George Washington, who proclaimed November 26, 1789, as a day of public thanksgiving and prayer. In 1863

President Abraham Lincoln made Thanksgiving an official annual holiday and now each year there is a presidential proclamation setting the fourth Thursday in November as Thanksgiving Day.

Besides having a big turkey dinner with your family and friends, what does this holiday mean today? After all, there's enough food in the supermarket to help us survive the winter. We don't have to depend only on the food we grow ourselves and we don't usually think about being thankful for this year's harvest.

But there are many other things to be thankful for. No matter where you live or how rich or poor you are, you no doubt have something you feel good about. Maybe you think your family is more terrific than any other family you know. That's something to be thankful for. Perhaps last year was a terrible one in school and you're grateful that this year is so much better. Or maybe just knowing you have good friends makes you happy.

Thanksgiving is a good day to think over the pluses in your life and to let people know you appreciate them.

Did You Know . . . ?

Thanksgiving Day used to be on the last Thursday in November. But in 1939 the country was still emerging from the Depression and businesses were struggling to survive. That year President Franklin D. Roosevelt changed Thanksgiving Day to the fourth Thursday so that there would be a longer shopping season before Christmas. (Actually, in most years the fourth Thursday in November is also the last Thursday in that month.)

*

How could the Pilgrims learn about new crops from the Native Americans who lived in Massachusetts? How could they communicate? The answer lies in the histories of two men, Samoset and Squanto. Samoset was a Pemaquid from Maine, and he had learned English from sailors on English fishing ships. He was the first to meet the Pilgrims and he told them about Squanto, who lived with the Wampanoags nearby. Squanto himself was a Pawtuxet who had been captured and taken to Europe, where he was sold as a slave. But he managed to escape and return home. There he found that the rest of the Pawtuxets had died in an epidemic. Squanto stayed with the Pilgrims for a long time and taught them many ways to survive in their new home.

*

Did you know that in Canada, Thanksgiving is celebrated on the second Monday in October? Perhaps this earlier date was chosen because Canada is farther north than the United States (except Alaska) and therefore its crops are harvested sooner than ours.

CELEBRATE!

Appreciation All Year Round

Let people know that you think they're great; at the same time, give them something to be thankful for themselves. Hand out "Thank You for Being You" coupons to members of your family and others you feel close to, like the neighbor who lets everyone play ball in her yard and the one who bakes cookies for you and your family.

The coupons you make and give to people are guarantees that you'll do something for them. For example, you might give your little brother a coupon he can cash in whenever he wants; in return he'll get an hour of your time to play games with him or help him build a Lego town. Moms and dads always appreciate help around the house; you could give them coupons worth five nights of dishwashing or three sessions with the vacuum cleaner or two free car washes by you. And what would please Grandma and Grandpa most might be some time alone with you, without the rest of the family around; treat them to a couple of afternoons with you at the local park or just chatting and playing cards.

You'll come up with your own ideas—anything from shoveling snow to baby-sitting to sewing up a hem or baking a pie. Once you've got your list together, all you need is some paper and a pen. Cut dollar-bill-sized coupons out of construction paper and write your message on them. Everyone will be really thankful to get them.

THANKS FOR BEING A GREAT *(dad, mom, uncle, etc.)*
This entitles _____ *(name)* _____
to 2 free carwashes, including vacuuming the inside.
Redeemable any weekend.

(sign your name)

Extras for the Feast

Most families serve traditional foods every year on Thanksgiving—turkey with stuffing, cranberry sauce, mashed and sweet potatoes, and pumpkin or squash pie are some examples of popular Thanksgiving goodies. However, especially when lots of people will be at the feast, it's nice to have some extras for those who don't care for some of the traditional items or just for the sake of having something new and different. Here are two very easy additions to the holiday meal that you can make; then sit back and listen to the *oh*s and *ah*s of appreciation.

Three-bean salad

Nothing could be simpler to make than this salad, and it's very tasty too. You need one can each of three different kinds of beans: lima beans, wax beans, green beans, garbanzo beans, white or red kidney beans, pink beans (you get the idea). Open the cans, drain off the liquid, dump the beans into a big bowl, add a half cup or so of Italian or oil-and-vinegar dressing, and stir. Then put it in the refrigerator until you're ready to eat.

Of course you can get fancy and add other things, such as: a can of whole-kernel corn (drained), chopped onion, chopped celery, chopped green or red pepper, and a sprinkle of parsley, chive, or dill. Plain or fancy, three-bean salad might become a new Thanksgiving tradition at your house.

Ambrosia

Ambrosia is a refreshing, light dessert, perfect for people who are too full for pie. You need 4 large oranges (seedless if possible), 4 bananas, and 1/4 cup of shredded coconut. First peel the oranges, pull the sections apart, and cut each section in half. Then peel and slice the bananas. Mix the fruit together in a bowl and sprinkle the coconut on top. Put it in the refrigerator until you're ready for dessert. This amount serves eight people.

If you want to make your ambrosia a little different, you can add a can of crushed pineapple or pineapple chunks to the fruit mixture (be sure to drain off the juice first). And if you're using a glass bowl, you can layer the fruit instead of mixing it together. Put a layer of orange pieces on the bottom, then make a layer of banana slices, and end with a layer of pineapple. Sprinkle coconut on top. The layers look nice through the glass sides of the bowl. But layered or mixed, this light and tangy dessert tastes great after turkey.

Presenting Winter

In the Northern Hemisphere the winter solstice occurs on about December 22. This is the first day of winter—the shortest day of the year. (Remember that winter in the Northern Hemisphere is summer in the Southern Hemisphere.)

How does this happen? Because the earth revolves around the sun at an angle, days vary in length through the year. North of the Equator, as the winter solstice approaches, there are fewer hours of sunlight each day. And the farther north you are, the shorter the days are. (Of course, south of the Equator the days are getting longer as December 22 approaches.) The Northern Hemisphere's winter solstice is the day when the sun is directly overhead at noon at the Tropic of Capricorn, which lies 23½ degrees south of the Equator.

Since human society began, people have noticed that there is a shortest day in the year. It must have been frightening to watch the days grow shorter and shorter; people must have wondered if this year the sun was going to disappear entirely. Without it their food crops wouldn't grow and the people themselves would die of cold. It's not surprising that they asked their gods to bring back the sun and gave thanks when the days started getting longer. Bonfires and torches were part of many ancient winter religious festivals, providing hope that the sun's light would return.

Purim

Purim is one of the most festive holidays for Jews, and children have a lot of fun on this day. Purim commemorates a story about the Jews in ancient Persia. Haman, the chief deputy of King Ahasuerus, planned to kill the Jews. But Queen Esther, who was Jewish, uncovered his plot and arranged that Haman himself would be hanged instead. On Purim Jews act out the story of Queen Esther. In many places people eat small triangular pastries called *hamantaschen* whose shape reminds them of Haman's hat.

Christianity

There are about 1.7 billion Christians today, making Christianity the most widely followed religion in the world. It began with Jesus, who lived about two thousand years ago in what is now Israel. (The calendar used in most of the world divides time into B.C., meaning "before Christ," and A.D. or *anno Domini*, which means "in the year of our Lord" in Latin.)

Jesus was a Jew who spoke to others about his beliefs; he criticized the religious leaders of the time and preached love and justice among all people, especially the poor and oppressed. The New Testament of the Bible describes the stories he told, called parables, that embodied his ideas; it also tells of many miracles he performed.

Some Jews believed that Jesus was the Messiah, a son of God sent to earth to bring peace and love to humanity (*Christ* is the Greek word for "Messiah," so *Jesus Christ* means "Jesus the Messiah"). These disciples followed him, helping to spread his message. Eventually Jesus was arrested by Jewish leaders and crucified by their Roman rulers. On the third day after he died, his tomb was found empty and his followers believed that he had been raised from the dead. The cross on which Jesus was crucified is Christianity's most important symbol.

Christians, like Jews, believe there is only one God, but the Christian God is a trinity made up of three parts: God, the father; Jesus Christ, his son; and the Holy Spirit, the unseen aspect of God that is present everywhere in the world. They believe that Jesus was sent by God to redeem the sins of all people through his death and that he lives forever in Heaven to help and comfort humanity.

After Jesus' death, Christianity spread and eventually an organized church system developed. As centuries passed, some Christian groups formed their own separate churches, still Christian but differing on various issues. Today there are about three hundred different Christian denominations, each with its own priests or ministers and its own style of worship.

Christmas

Christmas, a major Christian holiday, comes on December 25, soon after the winter solstice. It celebrates the birth of Jesus. (Some Eastern Orthodox Christians celebrate Christmas on January 7, because they use the old Julian calendar established by Julius Caesar in the year 46 B.C.; the date of December 25 for Christmas is according to the Gregorian calendar introduced by Pope Gregory XIII in 1582.)

The Bible says that Jesus was the son of God and that he was born to a woman named Mary. She and her husband Joseph had traveled to Bethlehem to be counted in a tax census; they couldn't find anyplace to stay, so Jesus was born in a stable. The night before his birth, a bright star was seen over the stable and an angel announced the birth of a savior to shepherds in the fields. Three kings followed the star to the stable and gave gifts to the baby when they arrived twelve days later.

This story is remembered at Christmas, when Christians go to church and celebrate at home with family and friends.

In the United States most Christians give gifts to children and friends on Christmas (in some other countries people give gifts on other days near Christmas). Santa Claus, based on Saint Nicholas, became a popular figure in the nineteenth century, and the idea that this magical person brings presents to children adds to the holiday's fun and excitement. Christmas carols, decorated trees, and a Christmas feast make this a joyous celebration.

Islam

Islam has about 750 million followers, who are called Muslims; *Islam* means "peace through submission to God" in Arabic, the main language of Islam, and *Muslim* means "one who submits." *Allah* is the word for "God" in Arabic; Muslims, like Jews and Christians, believe that there is only one God.

Islam began with Muhammad, who was born in A.D. 570 in Mecca, a city in today's Saudi Arabia. Muslims believe that when Muhammad was forty years old, the Archangel Gabriel spoke to him; the angel's words, repeated by Muhammad, became the first verses of the Qur'an, Islam's holy book. The angel continued to reveal Allah's word to Muhammad, and he continued to tell others about it. In 622 Muhammad fled to Medina, because people who didn't believe in the new religion he preached were plotting to kill him. From then until his death in 632, Muhammad's influence grew, and in 630 his followers returned to take over Mecca.

The basis of Islam is submission to God in every aspect of a person's life. There are five essential rules for Muslims: 1) to say "There is no god but Allah, and Muhammad is his prophet"; 2) to pray five times each day, facing Mecca, Islam's holy city; 3) to give generously to the poor; 4) to fast during the daytime in the month of Ramadan; 5) to make a pilgrimage to Mecca, if possible, once during one's lifetime.

Building on Judaism and Christianity, Islam says that

Muhammad was the last and greatest of a series of prophets; the others were Adam, Noah, Abraham, Moses, and Jesus. Muhammad is believed to be a descendant of Abraham through his son Ishmael, while Jews and therefore Christians are descended from Abraham through Isaac. The Qur'an tells Muslims how to live their lives, instructing them to honor their parents, help the poor, be honorable and just, and submit to Allah. Friday is the day of rest for Muslims; many go to mosques to pray and hear sermons on this day.

Like other major religions, Islam over the centuries has given rise to many different sects. But all of them follow the basic principles set down by Muhammad.

Ramadan

Ramadan is the ninth month of the Islamic calendar. It does not fall at the same time every year, because the Islamic year is based on the cycles of the moon, rather than on the earth's movement around the sun; this means that the Islamic year is about eleven days shorter than the solar year. For example, if Ramadan begins at the end of February one year, in three years it will begin about thirty-three days earlier, sometime near the end of January. It takes about thirty-three years for Ramadan to move backward through all the seasons and get back to the same time of the year.

Ramadan is the month during which Muhammad received the revelations from the Archangel Gabriel; it is also the month when Muhammad's army defeated the soldiers of Mecca in the Battle of Badr. Muslims must fast from sunrise to sunset for the whole month of Ramadan as a sign of their submission to Allah.

At the end of Ramadan many Muslims celebrate a festival called 'Id al-Fitr, which may last for three days. Families and friends gather to pray and to exchange gifts. Feasts and visiting friends make this a festive time, as Muslims exchange greetings of " 'Id mubarak" ("happy 'Id").

Hajj

Every Muslim who can must make one pilgrimage to Mecca. The pilgrimage, called the Hajj, should be made during the last Islamic month, Dhul-hijja; if it is made at a different time of year, it has a different name. The Hajj is the most important event in a Muslim's life, and people save their money for years in preparation for it.

As the date approaches, pilgrims pour into Mecca. They must wear special clothing for the Hajj. The pilgrims perform rituals that take about five days; they may also visit holy places in Medina. Before they go home, many pilgrims drink water from a holy well, and they may take some of it home for their families.

When pilgrims return home from the Hajj, they are congratulated and treated with respect for having fulfilled this important duty of Islam.

December 26–January 1

Kwanzaa

Kwanzaa is an African-American holiday that was established in 1966. The word *kwanzaa* means "first fruits" in Swahili, a language spoken in many African countries. The holiday is based on festivals in Africa that celebrate the gathering of crops that will feed the community.

But Kwanzaa is more than a harvest festival. It is a time for Americans of African descent to come together to celebrate their history and culture and to honor their ancestors. Kwanzaa is a community holiday, during which people reach out to their neighbors and friends and think about their shared beliefs and values.

These beliefs and values are summed up in the seven principles of Kwanzaa:

umoja = unity
kujichagulia = self-determination
ujima = collective work and
   responsibility

ujamaa = cooperative
   economics
nia = purpose
kuumba = creativity
imani = faith

The ideas behind these principles are quite complicated, but taken all together, they emphasize working together for the benefit of everyone in the community and believing in the strength that such working together produces.

During Kwanzaa, homes and community buildings are decorated in red, black, and green. A straw mat called a *mkeka* is placed on a low table; it symbolizes the traditions of Africa as the basis of African-American culture. A candleholder, or *kinara*, is set in the center of the *mkeka*. On each night of Kwanzaa a candle is lit to symbolize one of the seven principles. On December 31 there is a feast or *karamu*; everyone gathers to eat good food and enjoy one another's company, and there may be music and dancing and traditional storytelling.

Kwanzaa is not a religious holiday; it's a celebration that focuses on family and friends and on the ties that hold them together.

Did You Know . . . ?

Maulana Karenga, a civil rights leader and teacher, started the idea of celebrating Kwanzaa in the United States. He thought it was important for black Americans to learn more about the African cultures that their ancestors came from. He also thought that black communities should have a holiday that held special meaning for them.

*

When a brand-new holiday is started, people often don't know exactly how they want to celebrate it. There are no special traditions that everyone has known since childhood (like trick-or-treating on Halloween or wearing green on St. Patrick's Day). But as more and more people learned about Kwanzaa and began to observe it, new traditions began to grow up. Now there are Kwanzaa cards, special Kwanzaa stories for young children, and Kwanzaa decorations; celebrations are held at many community centers, museums, and schools. And of course, with a new holiday, everyone gets to have the fun of starting new traditions for family and friends.

*

Swahili is not the language of any one ethnic group in Africa. It is a language that developed after Arab traders began to settle on Africa's eastern coast and to intermarry with the people already living there. Swahili became known as a "trade language," one used by traders who traveled through much of Africa. Today it is spoken by many people in eastern Africa, usually in addition to their own tribal language. So, for instance, a Kikuyu might be able to talk with a Masai only in Swahili.

CELEBRATE!

Make a Mkeka

The *mkeka* or straw mat that is used in Kwanzaa celebrations reminds people of the intricately woven baskets and mats that are found throughout Africa. It's fun and very easy to make a woven mat yourself; by using paper instead of straw, you may feel you are combining a tradition of African culture with familiar products of your own American life.

You can use straw-colored construction paper for your mat—maybe tan or pale yellow or pale green, or a combination of these. Or, if you prefer, use paper in the Kwanzaa colors of red, black, and green. Cut nice straight strips of the paper about 3/4" to 1" wide and as long as you want the mat to be. (Don't try to make it too big; about 8" by 8" is a good size.)

Start at one corner and lay a strip in each direction, overlapping the ends. Now lay a second strip in one direction, weaving it under. Keep adding strips, first in one direction and then in the other. The easiest way to put in each new strip is to arrange it over and under the open ends of the strips; then use your other hand to keep the already woven strips in place while you slide the new one into position.

When you're finished weaving and the strips are all nice and straight, you can put some tape across the corners of the mat on the underside; this will help hold it together. You

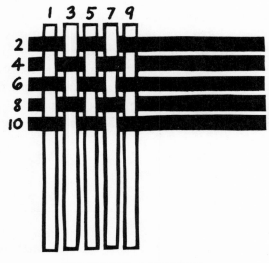

WEAVING A MKEKA

can fringe the edges of the mat if you want to make it look more like straw, or you can leave the edges smooth.

Now you're all ready to use your *mkeka* in your Kwanzaa celebrations.

Honoring Your Ancestors

One of the most important parts of Kwanzaa is paying honor to your ancestors, without whom you wouldn't even be here! But sometimes it's difficult to feel connected to people you never met and whose names you may not know. So why not introduce yourself to them and let them get to know you a little better?

If you have a tape recorder, you can make a tape for your ancestors and play it for the rest of the family at your Kwanzaa celebration. Be sure to be respectful as you begin; address your ancestors politely and introduce yourself with your name, your age, and any other information about yourself you think is important.

Now you have to decide what to say to your ancestors. What do you think might be most important to them? Perhaps they would care most about what kind of person you are and whether you are someone they could be proud to claim as a descendant. Think about what you have done in the year that has passed since the last Kwanzaa. What have you accomplished that has made you feel good about yourself? Maybe you've done well in school or in sports; maybe you've been a good friend to someone who needed your help; maybe you've learned to get along better with your brother or your parents.

But your ancestors probably would like to know what else happened this year—funny things, like when you put the milk away in the cupboard instead of the refrigerator; exciting things, like when you won a prize for guessing the number of jelly beans in a jar; even sad things, like when you broke your arm and couldn't play basketball for two months.

As you make your "ancestor tape," you'll probably think of things you've almost forgotten. Remembering the year that's just finished and talking about it on your tape may make you realize how much you've changed in that year and how much you've learned. That can be a good feeling!

Note: If you don't have a tape recorder that works, you can write a letter to your ancestors and read it out loud at the family Kwanzaa celebration. This can seem harder than playing a tape you've already prepared—but everyone will be proud of you for doing it.

Gather a Kwanzaa Harvest

Since Kwanzaa is based on African holidays that celebrate the gathering of the harvest, it's fun to make harvest baskets of your own to decorate your home or classroom. In most parts of the United States, of course, December and January are not harvest months, but there are lots of fruits available in the markets that you can use. Remember that the Kwanzaa colors are black, red, and green. Why not use a black basket or other container and fill it with red and green apples?

Paint a basket or other container (such as a cookie tin)

black, or cover the inside and outside of the container with black construction paper or fabric. Then use narrow ribbon or yarn to tie red bows on the stems of the green apples and green bows on the stems of the red apples. If you have extra ribbon or yarn, twist the two colors together and tie a bow around the basket itself.

For a smaller decorative piece, try filling a small basket or bowl with nuts whose shells are painted red, green, and black. Your harvest baskets will look attractive and will remind family and friends of the origins of this holiday.

January 1

New Year's Day

Wouldn't it be great if you could erase all the mistakes you made and the bad things that happened last year? Then you could start over again and do everything right this time! And New Year's is the perfect day to begin.

Everywhere in the world people celebrate the end of an old year and the arrival of a new one. This doesn't come at the beginning of January for everyone. It is celebrated in the fall in the Jewish calendar and in late winter or spring by many Asian cultures. But the official New Year's Day in the United States and much of the world is January 1.

January was named after the Roman god Janus. He was always shown with two faces, symbolizing his connection with both beginnings and endings. On January 1 Janus looks back at the old year and forward to the new one that is about to start. And we do the same thing. You've probably seen the new year represented as a new baby and the old year as an old man leaning on a stick. Lots of people stay up past midnight on December 31 to celebrate the very beginning of the new year.

People seem to feel the need to start fresh from time to time and New Year's is a convenient occasion. We all wish the bad things of the past year had never happened, and we look for a way to wipe them out and start with a clean slate. Often quarrels are forgiven and the two people decide to forget their disagreement and start afresh. And we are all reminded to forgive and forget with traditional New Year's Eve songs like "Auld Lang Syne" (this means "the good old days" in an old Scots dialect).

As we say goodbye to the old year, we think about what we want to do differently and make New Year's resolutions that will begin on January 1. Some people resolve to live up to their promises in a way they haven't done in the past. Lots of people resolve to improve their lives—by exercising more often, eating less junk food, getting things done on time. Still others resolve to learn a new skill, get a new job, or do better in school.

Of course resolutions are much easier to make than to keep. But the process of thinking about how you want to change your life for the better can sometimes get you going. And there's always another chance on next New Year's Day.

Did You Know . . . ?

The Tournament of Roses Parade in Pasadena, California, has been a New Year's Day tradition since 1886. Millions of people watch it in person or on television. The early years of the Rose Parade featured carriages and buggies decorated with flowers. Today, of course, there are huge, elaborate parade floats. Each float is completely covered with thousands of fresh flowers, which are carefully attached by hand before the parade begins. Prizes are given to the best floats in various categories, and after the parade there is a chance for people to take a closer look at the floats and their floral designs. High school and other marching bands as well as groups on horseback also take part in the Rose Parade, but the main attraction is the floats.

That afternoon one of the biggest college football games

of the year is played at the Rose Bowl, not far from the parade route.

*

Another famous parade is held every New Year's Day. It is the Mummers' Parade in Philadelphia, Pennsylvania. String bands, whose members do precision marching as they play, are the main attraction. The musicians wear incredibly elaborate costumes that use feathers, sequins, brightly colored satin and velvet, and huge headdresses. The string bands work in secret all year to create their costumes and marching routines so they will be a surprise on the day of the parade. Prizes are awarded for the best bands each year.

*

Lots of superstitions have grown up around the beginning of the new year. "First footing" means the first person to enter the house after midnight on New Year's Eve. In some places it is considered lucky for a dark-haired man to be the "first footer," while in others a fair-haired man is lucky.

In Scotland, when you enter a person's house for the first time in the new year, you should bring a lump of coal and a piece of bread so your friends will be warm and well fed in the coming year. Eating twelve grapes at New Year's brings good luck in the next twelve months in Spain. And in the southern United States, it's good luck to eat black-eyed peas on New Year's Day.

CELEBRATE!

Resolutions the Easy Way

Making resolutions is easy, but sometimes keeping them is hard work. Here's a way to add some fun to New Year's resolutions all year long.

Create a Resolution Grab Bag for yourself. On New Year's Day decide on twelve ways you'd like to improve yourself in the new year. These will be your resolutions. You might want to stop biting your nails or begin speaking up more in class.

Maybe you need to work on getting to school on time or not teasing your kid brother so much. Maybe you really want to learn to knit or get your baseball card collection organized, but you've never gotten around to doing it. This could be the year to try.

When you've got twelve, write each one on a long slip of paper. Roll each paper slip around a pencil with the writing on the inside and then slide it off. Tie each of these little "scrolls" with a ribbon or piece of string and then put the resolution scrolls in a small basket or box.

On the first day of each month you will pull out one of the scrolls and open it. That will be the resolution you'll try to keep for that month. But wait—you need one more scroll for good luck. Make another scroll that says "You're already doing great" or "Take it easy this month" or whatever works for you. Add this scroll to your box or basket. You'll have twelve chances to draw this good luck scroll.

Welcome the New Year with a Party

New Year's Eve and New Year's Day are times when lots of people want to have parties, and it's fun to say goodbye to the old year and welcome in the new one with people you like. Why not invite a few friends for a New Year's gathering?

Bake a lucky cake

Here's a way to make eating cake a game of chance, as everyone wonders who will get the piece that contains the lucky walnut. Bake whatever cake you like best (choose one without nuts) from a mix or from scratch; get an adult to help before you turn on the oven. Just before you put the cake in to bake, push half a walnut into the batter; make sure it sinks down enough so you can't see it. When your guests eat their cake, tell them to chew carefully—whoever gets the walnut will have good luck all year!

Wassail to drink

In the British Isles wassail, a hot drink of spiced ale, was served at New Year's, and many people today still serve hot drinks of various kinds at this holiday. A delicious kind of "wassail" is very easy to make. Pour a bottle or two of apple juice into a large pot and turn the heat on low (make sure you have permission to use the stove). Add two or three cinnamon sticks, a few whole cloves, a handful of raisins or currants, and a tablespoonful of brown sugar. Let the wassail get warm, but don't allow it to boil. The word *wassail* comes from ancient Norse words meaning "be healthy." So serve your wassail in cups and toast one another's good health as you drink it.

January, third Monday

Martin Luther King Day

Martin Luther King, Jr., was born on January 15, 1929; this movable holiday celebrates his birthday. King was a minister, an activist for civil rights, and a passionate believer in non-violent action for social change. Beginning in the 1950s he led demonstrations and marches, helped organize boycotts, and made powerful speeches that awakened many Americans to the injustices in our society. He believed that violence was never justified and that it only caused more violence; he believed that people should disobey laws that were unjust, as long as they were willing to accept the legal consequences (such as a fine or a jail term) of that disobedience; and he believed that voting was the most powerful way to make changes happen.

In 1963 Martin Luther King, Jr., along with other civil rights leaders, organized a demonstration that was called the March on Washington for Jobs and Freedom. About 250,000 people came to Washington, D.C., to show their support for the civil rights bill that Congress was considering. They stood in front of the Lincoln Memorial and listened as King spoke the passionate words that would echo through the whole country:

I have a dream that one day this nation will rise up and live out the true meaning of its creed: "We hold these truths to be self-evident, that all men are created equal."

I have a dream that one day on the red hills of Georgia the sons of former slaves and the sons of former slave-owners will be able to sit down together at the table of brotherhood. . . .

I have a dream that my four little children will one day live in a nation where they will not be judged by the color of their skin but by the content of their character.

I have a dream today.

I have a dream that one day . . . little black boys and black girls will be able to join hands with little white boys and white girls as sisters and brothers.

I have a dream today. . . .

When we let freedom ring, when we let it ring from every village and every hamlet, from every state and every city, we will be able to speed up that day when all of God's children, black men and white men, Jews and Gentiles, Protestants and Catholics, will be able to join hands and sing in the words of the old Negro spiritual, "Free at last! Free at last! Thank God almighty, we are free at last!"

King's speech, made in 1963, still has the power to stir our emotions and rouse us to work however we can to make our society a better and fairer one. And though many things Martin Luther King, Jr., worked for have come true, there is still much of his dream that is not yet realized. Martin Luther King Day is a time to think about what this extraordinary man accomplished and how we can continue his work.

Did You Know . . . ?

Martin Luther King, Jr., first became nationally known because of the Montgomery, Alabama, bus boycott in 1955. At that time Montgomery's laws said black people had to ride in the back sections of buses and had to give up their seats to white passengers. When a black woman, Rosa Parks, was arrested for refusing to give up her seat to a white person, Martin Luther King, Jr., helped to organize a boycott of the buses by black people. After the boycott had gone on for almost a year, the United States Supreme Court declared Montgomery's law about bus seating unconstitutional.

*

Martin Luther King, Jr., was assassinated in Memphis, Tennessee, on April 4, 1968. He had gone to Memphis to support a strike by sanitation workers, most of whom were black. His violent death shocked people, and thousands who knew him only through his speeches and courageous actions went to Atlanta, Georgia, for his funeral. President Lyndon Johnson ordered that flags on all government buildings be flown at half-staff as a mark of respect for this great leader.

*

Martin Luther King Day was made an official holiday in 1983, when Congress approved a bill "to make Martin Luther King's birthday a legal public holiday." The bill was signed by President Ronald Reagan in November 1983; it sets the third Monday in January as the holiday.

CELEBRATE!

Dreams for a Better World

Martin Luther King, Jr., never gave up on his dreams for a better world. And he spoke about his dreams in words that touched other people deeply. On Martin Luther King Day, it's good to listen to a recording of his "I Have a Dream" speech of 1963. After you hear it, you can think about what your dreams are—for America, for your community, or for your family and yourself. What would make things better for the people of this country and the world?

Share your dreams

Write down your own dreams; use words that tell clearly what you hope to see happen. Try to describe your dream in ways that will make people feel the same way you do. When you're happy with what you have written, copy it neatly on a clean sheet of paper with the heading "I Have a Dream."

Share your dreams with the other people in your class. Do you all have the same ideas of how to improve things? Do some people have ideas you never would have thought of? Can you think of ways to make any of these dreams come true?

Spread the word

Perhaps there are a few dreams that your whole class agrees on. Martin Luther King Day is the perfect time to tell other people about these dreams. Write them out neatly and have everyone in the class sign his or her name at the bottom. You might want to add the name of your school, your town, and what grade you're in.

Then send your dreams to your local newspaper. Write a polite letter explaining why you've been talking about your dreams for your town or for the whole country. Address it to the "Letters to the Editor," and perhaps you will see your dreams in print.

Tell the world

To tell more people about your hopes for the world, you can send your dreams to the government officials who represent you. You might send them to your senators, your congressional representative, or local officials such as the mayor of your town or other people who are elected. It is helpful to politicians to know what the people they represent are thinking about. Martin Luther King Day is a good time to remind your representatives of the problems that still need to be solved and to tell them your ideas for making things better.

Steps on the Road to Civil Rights

It's hard to imagine that in fairly recent history—in your own parents' lifetime—people in the United States were killed over the issue of whether blacks could participate in everyday activities along with white people. But in some parts of our country blacks really were not allowed by law to use "white" drinking fountains, sit at "white" lunch counters in dime stores, sit in "white" sections of movie theaters, and sit on a bus if white people were standing.

Things are different now, but it's important to remember what happened back then, so we can make sure it doesn't happen again. And it's important to remember those people who lost their lives in the struggle for civil rights.

One way to do this is to make a long scroll showing some of the major events of the civil rights era. This is a great project for the whole class. You'll need marker pens and a roll of paper—plain shelf paper or brown paper will work fine. Make a list of the events you all agree are important, and enter them carefully on your scroll. You can add pictures of people and places; you can also add quotes from Dr. King's speeches.

When your scroll is finished, hang it in the hall or the school lobby so everyone can read it and think about what it means.

February 2

Groundhog Day

Almost everyone has heard of Groundhog Day. That's the date on which a groundhog (also known as a woodchuck) comes out of his hole and predicts the weather for the next six weeks. Of course he doesn't use a moving map for his predictions, the way television weather reporters do. But many people are sure that if the groundhog sees his shadow when he pops out of his hole on February 2, there will be six more weeks of bad winter weather. If the sky is overcast and he doesn't see his shadow, then the weather should be mild and spring will be earlier.

The most famous groundhog is Punxsutawney Phil. He lives near the small north central Pennsylvania town of Punxsutawney. Every year people of the town, television reporters, and tourists gather around Phil's heated bunker on Gobbler's Knob to find out what the weather for the next six weeks will be. The members of the Punxsutawney Groundhog Club say that in more than ninety years of weather predicting, Phil has never been wrong.

No one knows for sure when people began celebrating Groundhog Day. A Pennsylvania storekeeper wrote about it in his diary in 1841 and many people believe that the custom originated with early German settlers in that part of the United States. In other countries similar legends exist. Many Germans think that a badger predicts the weather, and in France and England some people rely on a bear. But none of these other animal weather forecasters is as well known as Punxsutawney Phil.

Groundhog Day is one of those homegrown American holidays that's based on folk traditions and good fun. No matter what part of the country you live in, you can enjoy the suspense of wondering how long winter will last this year.

Did You Know . . . ?

The people of Punxsutawney are very proud of their groundhog Phil and have a big ceremony for his appearance on Groundhog Day. The head of the Punxsutawney Groundhog Club dresses up in tailcoat and striped pants, as if he's going to a formal ball. He leads everyone up to Phil's burrow and raps on it with a special acacia-wood cane. He says he talks to Phil in groundhog language; then he tells everyone what Phil said. If you watch the evening news on television on February 2, you'll probably get to see Phil, but the television microphones usually can't catch what he says.

*

A number of other towns and cities would like to have a groundhog as famous as Phil. In New York City there was a contest to name the city's official groundhog. The name they chose was Pothole Pete. But even a funny name hasn't helped him become a once-a-year television star like Phil.

How many Phils, and sons and daughters of Phil, do you think there have been over the years?

CELEBRATE!

Back to the Future with a Groundhog?

Often a time capsule is put inside the cornerstone of a new town hall or library that's being built. Inside the time capsule are items that tell what it's like living today so that when people open the capsule fifty or a hundred years from now, they'll know what everyday life was like.

You can make your own time capsule, and you don't need to wait one hundred years to open it! Decide on how long you want it to stay sealed—three months, six months, or even a year. By the time you open it up, you may have already forgotten what your favorite song was way back then. Time capsules are a fun way of remembering how things were and of seeing how accurately you can make predictions about coming events.

To make a time capsule, you'll need a container—maybe a shoebox. First put in things that tell what it's like where you live right now: the front page of today's newspaper and maybe an ad or two for stuff you buy; a list of your favorite colors and songs and sports; the names of your best friends. You should write a paragraph or two about who you are, where you live, what grade you're in. Include your teacher's name, and maybe which subjects are your favorites.

Now write down some predictions. Remember that you get to decide when your time capsule will be opened. Be sure that your predictions are about things that will take place during the time the capsule is sealed. Maybe you'd like to guess who will be your teacher next year or which team will win the World Series or who your best friend will be then. You might even want to guess what the weather will be, like Punxsutawney Phil.

Seal your time capsule with tape and on the outside write the date you sealed it and the date you're supposed to open it. No fair peeking. Before long you'll find out whether your predictions came true. And if your friends make time capsules too, you can compare predictions and see who was the best groundhog.

Test Your Prediction Skills

No matter where you live, there's no absolutely certain way to predict what the average temperature and rainfall will be for the next six weeks. Even Phil isn't that specific. But you and a friend can have a contest to see who can come the closest. All you need are a few household items and a piece of paper for recording the daily results.

First of all, each of you should write down what you think the average temperature outside your house will be in the next six weeks. Next estimate the daily average of rain or snowfall you'll have during the same amount of time. If you think there won't be any, write "none." But if you think there might be just a little bit, too little to measure with a ruler, write "scant." Otherwise, write down your guess to the nearest eighth of an inch. Remember, you're predicting the daily average, not the total.

To measure daily rainfall, you'll need a rain gauge. Use a fairly wide glass or clear-plastic peanut butter jar or any other jar with straight sides. Set it in a bucket so it won't tip over in case there's a gust of wind, and put the bucket outside to

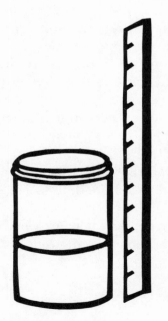

MEASURING RAIN IN A RAINFALL GAUGE

catch any rain that falls. Be sure you don't put your rain gauge under an overhang that will keep the rain away from it or under trees that will drip extra water into it and spoil your accuracy.

You'll need to measure the amount of precipitation every day at the same time; and it's a good idea to do it in the morning, before the day's sun evaporates any water that's collected in your rain gauge. Hold a small ruler up to the outside of the jar every day and write down the water depth to the nearest eighth of an inch. If there's too little to measure, write either "none" or "scant," depending on whether it rained at all that day. Some jars have thick bottoms that can mess up your measurements; look through the glass to see where the water actually begins and measure from there. When you're finished measuring, throw out the water and put your rain gauge back in the same spot.

All you need for a temperature gauge is a regular outdoor thermometer. Be sure it's not hanging in the sun, because that will throw off your reading. Look at the temperature each day at the same time and write down the results.

At the end of six weeks, add up the temperatures and divide by the number of days you recorded. Do the same with the rainfall. If all your rainfall records say "scant" and "none," look to see which of those occurred most often—that's another way to take an average.

You can match your predicting skills with a friend who lives in a different town or even a different part of the country. After all, your prediction is for what's going to happen at your house; hers will be for where she lives. The question is, whose guess is closest to what really happened?

Decide on a prize for the best weather predictor before you begin. A rain hat or a pair of plastic sunglasses might be appropriate!

February 14

Valentine's Day

Valentine's Day has been celebrated for centuries, and it's especially popular in England, France, Canada, and the United States. But though everyone knows what Valentine's Day means—love, friendship, pretty cards, flowers—no one is quite sure how it got started or why it's called Valentine's Day.

It may have been named after a Christian named Valentine. According to legend, he was imprisoned by the Romans in about A.D. 270 because he would not give up his Christian beliefs. The daughter of his jailer became his friend, and Valentine wrote her a note before he was executed and signed it "Your Valentine." He later was made a saint; his feast day is February 14 and Valentine's Day is sometimes called St. Valentine's Day.

All kinds of traditions grew up as Valentine's Day was celebrated over the centuries. Even today, Valentines are often sent anonymously, signed only "Your Valentine." The symbols used on Valentine cards have a long history. A red heart, of course, is the most popular Valentine sign and it's easy to see where that one came from. Giving your heart to someone meant giving him or her the most important part of yourself.

Ribbons often decorate Valentines. Perhaps this came from the times when knights competed in tournaments. A knight's sweetheart often gave him a ribbon as a token of her love; the knight attached it to his lance for good luck. And what about lace? Of course it's pretty and delicate, just right for a Valentine, but the word *lace* comes from the Latin word *laqueus*, which means "a snare or noose." Maybe the lace on a Valentine is intended to snare someone's heart.

Sometimes all the emphasis on love and sweethearts makes it seem that Valentine's Day is only for people in love. But nowadays that's not true. It's a day to let anyone you care about—your parents, your other relatives, and your friends—know that you like them a lot. Sometimes a Valentine you make yourself means more than a card you could buy. And it's fun to use your imagination to dream up unusual Valentines for your friends and family.

Did You Know . . . ?

The idea of chance or luck has been part of Valentine's Day for hundreds of years. People used to think that the first person you saw on Valentine's Day morning would be your sweetheart. In the 1600s in England, wealthy people held a Valentine's Day lottery. Each woman drew a man's name from a bowl; that man was her Valentine and he was supposed to give her a Valentine present. She might be lucky one year and draw the name of a generous man known for his lavish gifts. If not, she could always hope for a luckier Valentine the next year. Valentine lotteries are still held in some schools, when students draw names of classmates to give Valentines to.

*

Who was Cupid, anyway, and how did he get involved with Valentine's Day? He was the god of love in ancient Roman mythology, and he was portrayed as a naked little boy with wings, carrying a bow and arrows. When Cupid shot an arrow at someone's heart, that person fell in love with whoever he or she was looking at. Cupid was a mischievous child who often played tricks, making people fall in love with the wrong person.

*

Did you ever wonder why birds, and especially doves, are often pictured on Valentine cards? Doves have long been associated with love; they were special to Venus and other love gods and goddesses in ancient times, and they have also been messengers since the times of Noah's ark. In the Middle Ages people noticed that some kinds of birds mated in February, and they knew that many birds, like doves and pigeons, mate with the same partner for their whole lives. So doves provided a good symbol of true, lifelong love that began in February as well as a messenger who brings a message of love, such as a Valentine.

CELEBRATE!

Valentines for Special People

Everybody likes to receive Valentines on February 14, and sometimes people feel left out and sad if they don't get any. This is especially true of people who don't have family or friends nearby. There's probably a nursing home in your town whose residents would be thrilled to get Valentines this year from young people like you and your friends. Other places where your class might send Valentines are shelters for the homeless, prisons, day-care centers for homeless kids, hospital wards, and army bases.

Obviously, sending a Valentine to someone you've never met isn't saying you love that person. But it's a way of saying you care about the whole human race and a way of cheering up someone who may be lonely or unhappy. Sign just your first name if you want to. Otherwise, sign it "Your Valentine" or "A Valentine Friend"—it can be fun for people to get anonymous cards on Valentine's Day.

This is a good project for your whole class to get involved

with. And it's a chance to make lots of different Valentines, each one more creative than the last. Hearts and lace doilies, ribbons and bows, and pictures of Cupids and flowers all make traditional Valentines that anyone will appreciate. Inside the card you can write just "Happy Valentine's Day" or use that old favorite, "Roses are red, Violets are blue, Sugar is sweet, And so are you."

Maybe you feel a humorous Valentine would be fun to make. See if your mom or dad has an old seed catalog with pictures of vegetables and fruits in it. Cut out a picture to go with one of those old Valentine jokes and paste it on the card. Inside write the joke: "My heart beets for you," "We make a great pear," "Peas be mine," or "Honey dew you care for me?" You'll come up with others as you brainstorm with your friends.

Ask your teacher to find out how these Valentines can be delivered. Then enjoy the good feeling that you've given a stranger a happy surprise.

Send a Secret Valentine

What about a really different kind of Valentine? If you think that some people you send Valentines to might consider flowers and lace too soppy, try Valentines in code to make them exercise their brains. It's not hard and it's fun to see how the three words "Happy Valentine's Day" look in various codes. First, try backward code: YADSENITNELAVYPPAH (leave out the apostrophe in your codes to make them harder to decipher). That long word looks pretty weird, and it's even weirder if you break it up into fake words: YADS ENIT NEL AVYP PAH.

Most people will decipher backward code pretty easily. If you want something trickier, use an alphabet substitution code. Write out the whole alphabet on a piece of paper; then write it again backward under the first alphabet, so A lines up with Z, B lines up with Y, and so on. Now all you do is find the letters that correspond to the ones in your message. HAPPY VALENTINE'S DAY becomes SZKKB EZOVMGRMVH WZB in this code. People may be able to decipher this code without any help, but just in case they can't, write it out on the back of the card. Sign your code Valentine "Your Secret Valentine" to add to the mystery.

If you know other codes, you might want to use them instead. And if you get really into it, you can write the whole "Roses are red" verse in code. Looks pretty strange, doesn't it?

Counting Hearts

The word *heart* is used in many common phrases in English, such as "Have a heart" and "His heart is in the right place." How many others can you come up with? Try making a list of phrases and expressions that contain the word *heart* and see if you know what they really mean. Does *heart* always mean the same thing in these expressions? What does "wearing your heart on your sleeve" mean, or "the heart of the matter"? You might want to post your list in the hall at school and invite other students to add to it.

February, third Monday

Presidents' Day

Presidents' Day honors two of America's best-known and beloved presidents, George Washington and Abraham Lincoln. Washington's real birthday was February 22, 1732, and Lincoln's was February 12, 1809. Both birthdays used to be celebrated as separate holidays, but now they are combined in one—Presidents' Day.

These two great men had many other things in common besides their February birthdays—things that made them stand out in their own times and that make us remember them today. They led the country through the two greatest upheavals it has ever had. Washington was commander-in-chief of the American troops during the Revolutionary War, when thirteen colonies broke away from England and formed a new nation. Lincoln was president when the Civil War began, a war that threatened to split apart the United States forever.

Both of these men held strong beliefs about freedom, justice, and the importance of standing up for what they believed was right. Their obvious fairmindedness helped each of them to bring together all kinds of very different people. But the quality they are both best known for is integrity.

95

It's interesting that the stories that grew up about the child-hoods of both Washington and Lincoln focus on their honesty. George Washington is supposed to have cut down a cherry tree; when his father asked if he had done it, George confessed, saying, "I cannot tell a lie." A story about Lincoln says that he borrowed a book, and when it got soaked with water, he worked three days shucking corn to repay the book's owner. Though these stories may not really be true, they emphasize the importance each man placed on keeping his word and telling the truth, and other people respected them for this quality.

Another connection links these two presidents. Lincoln once said, "Back in my childhood, I got hold of a small book, Weems's *Life of Washington*. I remember all the accounts there given of the battlefields and struggles for the liberties of the country. I recollect thinking then that there must have been something more than common that those men struggled for." Lincoln himself spent his presidency struggling for the liberties that make our country strong. Both Washington and Lincoln cared deeply about the ideals upon which the United States was founded and they gave their talents and energies to serving the country.

Did You Know . . . ?

George Washington and Abraham Lincoln were both very tall men. Washington was more than six feet in height, and Lincoln stood six feet four inches. Even today they would be above the average height. But when they were alive, they towered over most other men. In those days people didn't know as much about nutrition as we know now, and many people had very little variety in what they ate every day. The average height of people in early America was less than it is today.

*

Abraham Lincoln was probably the greatest speechmaker of any American president. The words of his Second Inaugural

Address, made at a time when the country knew the Civil War would soon be over, express compassion and hope for peace:

> With malice toward none; with charity for all; with firmness in the right, as God gives us to see the right, let us strive on to finish the work we are in; to bind up the nation's wounds; to care for him who shall have borne the battle, and for his widow and his orphan—to do all which may achieve and cherish a just and lasting peace among ourselves and with all nations.

Lincoln's address at Gettysburg, where a cemetery for soldiers had been made, is even more famous. It begins, "Fourscore and seven years ago our fathers brought forth on this continent a new nation conceived in liberty and dedicated to the proposition that all men are created equal," and ends, "We here highly resolve . . . that this nation under God shall have a new birth of freedom, and that government of the people, by the people, for the people, shall not perish from the earth." It's almost impossible to say these words aloud without feeling their power and the fervent beliefs that they represent. Their meaning is as important today as it was when they were first spoken.

*

George Washington was not the same kind of brilliant speechmaker that Lincoln was, and his own words are not nearly as well known to most people. He was a modest man whose actions spoke louder than words in the turmoil of war and the forming of a new nation. But words spoken about him by those who knew him have survived in the history books. Most people know that Washington was "First in war, first in peace, and first in the hearts of his countrymen." This was said by "Light-Horse Harry" Lee, who had fought with General Washington through the whole Revolutionary War. After Washington's death, Thomas Jefferson said, "He was indeed a wise, a good and a great man. His integrity was most pure; his justice the most inflexible I have ever known. He was incapable of fear, meeting personal dangers with the calmest unconcern." That's not a bad way to be remembered by your friends.

CELEBRATE!

Words Within Words

On Presidents' Day you'll probably learn some new information about George Washington and Abraham Lincoln in school. But here is a game that will teach you just how clever you are with words! Any number can play and all you need are pencil and paper.

Write the name WASHINGTON on the board or have each person write it at the top of his or her paper. Then start the timer. Each player has five minutes to write down as many words as possible, using only the letters in the name WASHINGTON. It's easy to see eight words (including wash, washing, and ton). But when you rearrange the letters, you'll find more.

You can make things more exciting by using both names, WASHINGTON and LINCOLN, or using GEORGE WASHINGTON or ABRAHAM LINCOLN. You can even use all four names if you're good at this. But be warned—the more letters you have to play with, the harder the game gets. You may want to give everyone ten minutes instead of five if you use all the names, because your list may be very long by the time you finish.

When the time is up, the person with the most words is the winner.

Play a Presidential Game

Here's another game that's good for a whole crowd. You need a sheet of notebook-size paper for each person. To get ready, make a list of all the presidents and their wives; use the names they're generally known by, such as Abraham Lincoln and Mary Todd Lincoln, and don't include James Buchanan because he was a bachelor!

The idea of the game is to attach a name of a president or his wife to the back of each player's shirt (use tape or safety pins). Then the players have to guess who they are and find their partners. They do this by asking yes-or-no questions that the other players must answer; the only question that can't be asked and answered, of course, is "Is my name _____?" That would make it too easy to figure out your name by just going down the list of presidents.

Choose half as many presidential couples as you have players. You may want to write down the dates of their births and deaths, or of their presidencies, along with their names to make answering the questions a little easier for everyone. Questions like "Am I alive now?" or "Was I alive during the Revolutionary War?" or "Was a relative of mine also a president?" will help you narrow down your name to a few possibilities. Remember, though, that the boys don't necessarily have presidents' names and the girls won't always be the wives.

When you think you know who you are, find your partner (you can read his or her name). Then announce, "We are George and Martha Washington" or whoever, and the other players will see if you are right. The first couple to figure out who they are wins.

February 29 (every fourth year)

Leap Year Day

In most years February has only twenty-eight days, but some years February 29 is on the calendar. This "extra" day is called Leap Year Day. And a year that has an extra day is called a leap year. This may seem a little odd. Why can't all the years have the same number of days?

It's because the earth doesn't take exactly 365 days to travel around the sun; it actually takes 365 days, 5 hours, 48 minutes, and about 46 seconds. Those extra hours and minutes add up to almost one whole day every four years. So every four years an extra day in February is on the calendar to even things out.

It took people a very long time to figure this out. Over the centuries there have been a number of different kinds of calendars with differing numbers of months and days. None of them worked very well until the time of Julius Caesar. In 46 B.C. he invented a new calendar that included the concept of leap year. But in his calendar, called the Julian calendar after him, the length of a year was calculated at 365 days and 6 hours.

Those few extra minutes every year (6 whole hours instead of a little more than 5¾ hours) kept adding up. By 1582 people who used this calendar were ten days ahead of themselves. In that year Pope Gregory XIII revised the Julian calendar by dropping ten days. To prevent this problem from happening again, he also decided that adding an extra day every four years was a little too much. In the Gregorian calendar, named after the Pope, every year that is divisible by four is a leap year except for century years that are not evenly divisible by four hundred. So, while 1992, 1996, and 2000 are leap years, the year 1900 was not because 1,900 can't be evenly divided by 400.

The Gregorian calendar is used in most parts of the world today, but it took quite a while for some countries to adopt it. England used the old Julian calendar until 1752. By that time it was eleven days off and when they switched over on September 2, 1752, the next day was September 14. (England's American colonies made the change at the same time.)

Even the Gregorian calendar isn't totally exact. But it is only off by twenty-six seconds a year. That will add up to an extra day by the year 4905, so there's not a lot for us to worry about.

Because it's kind of strange to have an extra day in the year, people have traditionally done things on Leap Year Day that they wouldn't normally do. For instance, it used to be that only men proposed marriage; the women had to wait until they were asked. But on Leap Year Day it was perfectly okay for a woman to propose to a man. Of course, he didn't have to say yes.

Leap Year Day is a great day to do something totally out of the ordinary and fun. Start thinking now about some unusual way to give yourself a treat next Leap Year Day.

Did You Know . . . ?

Since 1900 the earth's rotation around the sun has been slowing down. Don't worry—it's only slowed by a tiny bit. Scientists use atomic clocks that are incredibly accurate. An atomic second is slightly shorter than an astronomical second, which is based on the earth's rotation. So every now and then, since 1972, a leap second has been added to the atomic clock to keep it coordinated with the astronomical one. This second is added just before midnight, but even if you waited up to watch, you wouldn't notice a thing.

*

Do you know anyone whose birthday is on Leap Year Day? If you were born on February 29, you'd be four years old on your first birthday. A Leap Year Day baby would have only two birthdays by the time he was eight and four by the time he was old enough to vote at age eighteen. This doesn't sound like much fun. What about all the parties and presents that everyone else gets every year? If you're a Leap Year Day child, you've probably decided to celebrate your birthday on either February 28 or March 1 except in Leap Year.

*

Although the Gregorian calendar is recognized all over the world, it's not the only one that's used. For instance, Jews have their own calendar, one that does not date from the birth of Christ. The Gregorian year 2000 corresponds to the year 5760 in the Hebrew calendar. Since the Jewish New Year comes in the fall, their year 5760 starts in the fall of 1999. Jainism is a religion based in India. For Jains too, the new year starts in the fall; their year 2526 starts in the fall of 1999.

Chinese New Year, on the other hand, is in the late winter, and the Chinese also have their own calendar. The year 2000 is the year 4698 in the Chinese calendar; it is the seventeenth year of the seventy-eighth cycle and is known as the Year of the Dragon. Still another calendar is used in Muslim countries. The Islamic year 1378 is the year A.D. 2000, because Muslims begin counting the years from A.D. 622.

*

There are people who think that the Gregorian calendar we use is dumb. These people want to make up a new one. They say it's silly for months to have different numbers of days. Also, they think our current calendar makes it too difficult to figure out what day of the week a particular date will fall on. After all, in the Gregorian calendar months start on various days of the week and no date lands on the same day of the week in any two consecutive years.

In the 1930s a group called the World Calendar Association devised a "perpetual calendar." You can see that every year in this calendar would be exactly the same. January 1 would always be a Sunday, Valentine's Day would always be on Tuesday, and your birthday would always fall on the same day of the week.

In this calendar, each new quarter starts with a thirty-one-day month (January, April, July, October) and the rest all have thirty days. There are fifty-two weeks with seven days each, which adds up to 364 days. To deal with the 365th day, a "Worldsday" is added at the end of the year, on what would be December 31. It doesn't count as a Sunday—it's just Worldsday, a holiday for the whole world.

Of course, every four years something has to be done about leap year. To solve this problem, the World Calendar adds another Worldsday at the end of June. This one too doesn't count as a Sunday, and it's supposed to be a holiday for everyone to enjoy.

The World Calendar has been proposed as an idea that the United Nations should adopt, but many people objected to it and it didn't get very far. Maybe someone will bring it up again. What do you think of the idea?

CELEBRATE!

Be a Calendar Maker

People have been fiddling with different ways to arrange the calendar for centuries. So why not try it yourself and see if you can come up with a better arrangement than the one we're using? The only thing that's fixed is the number of days in the year, about 365¼. You can have as many months as you like and you can change the number of days in the week. For instance, you could have thirty weeks of twelve days each, with five days of vacation at the end of the year; however, you might have a hard time convincing people to work ten days without a weekend!

Leap Year Madness

Leap Year Day is super special because it comes along only once every four years. Why not take advantage of this rare occasion to do something outrageous and weird? Maybe your whole class would like to have a Leap Year celebration. Here are some ideas to get you started:

Tell everyone to wear their clothes inside out or backward on that day.

See if you can have your classes in backward order at school.

Be sure to eat your dinner in the morning and dessert before the main meal.

Have a backward spelling bee or a backward relay race. Of course, you'll start at the finish line.

By the time you're done with this inside-out-and-backward day, you'll probably be glad to get back to normal on March 1. It's a good thing Leap Year Day comes only once every four years!

March 11

Johnny Appleseed Day

Was Johnny Appleseed a real person or a legend, like Paul Bunyan? He was a real man and his real name was John Chapman. Not much is known about his early life except that he was born in Massachusetts in 1774 or 1775.

Apple seeds were brought from Europe by the early settlers and planted in the eastern colonies. Johnny Appleseed carried apple seeds from these colonies into what was then the wilderness of western Pennsylvania and Ohio. Wherever he found settlers, he planted his seeds so that in a few years the people would have apples to eat. He crisscrossed the frontier, planting new seeds and returning to tend the orchards that were growing up.

Everywhere he went, Johnny Appleseed was greeted with joy. Not only were apples a valuable food used for cider, cooking, and just plain eating, but the trees and blossoms reminded the lonely settlers of the homes they'd left behind back east.

Throughout his life Johnny Appleseed traveled a remarkable distance on foot. According to a number of accounts, he was seen as far west as Missouri and the Badlands of the Dakotas. He planted orchards in Michigan, Indiana, Ohio, Pennsylvania, and Kentucky.

He must have been a strange sight. His clothes were ragged and he was usually barefoot. He slept outdoors and wore his cooking pot on his head to keep his hands free to hold whatever book he was reading as he walked. Strangest of all, he never carried a gun in a time when people lived by hunting and were always prepared to defend themselves. He was renowned for never taking a life if he could help it, even an insect's. People said he talked to the animals and they responded by being his friends. And he made friends of settlers and Native Americans alike.

Johnny Appleseed lived to be more than seventy years old— perhaps his odd way of life was a healthy one. He died on March 11, 1847, and that is the date now celebrated as Johnny Appleseed Day.

Even without modern inventions like the telephone, radio, and television, word traveled fast about this strange but peace-loving man who brought the gift of apple orchards where they never had been before. A ragged stranger with few possessions who preferred camping out to sleeping in a house was an oddity even then, when there was lots of open space for such a man. How would he be greeted today, when most of the country is covered with roads and buildings? But there are still apple orchards in places like Indiana and Michigan, and perhaps they are descended from John Chapman's apple seeds.

Did You Know . . . ?

Lots of stories grew up about Johnny Appleseed, especially after an article about his life was published in 1871 in *Harper's New Monthly Magazine*. It's hard for us now to know how many of the legends are true. It was said that he met many people along the way who would later become very famous—people like the adventurous frontiersman Daniel Boone, the famous painter of American birds John J. Audubon, and even Abe Lincoln. And he might easily have met such men in the forests and small settlements he visited. It must have been an exciting time to live.

*

Johnny Appleseed was never without a sack of apple seeds and also never without a book. This too was a little strange out on the frontiers, where many people had no schools and never learned to read. Everywhere he went, he read aloud to people and encouraged them to read themselves. And one story says that a book actually saved his life. During the War of 1812 he warned the soldiers at a fort that Indians were about to attack a settlement nearby. He himself wouldn't lift a gun against either side, but he tried to help the wounded. As he did, a stray bullet hit him in the chest, but the thick book he was carrying inside his shirt stopped the bullet before it touched his skin.

*

In addition to apple trees, John Chapman planted herbs wherever he went. Most of the medicines we use today were unknown at that time and people relied on homemade medicines concocted from plants and herbs. Horehound was used for coughs, pennyroyal for fevers, and catnip for stomach pains and bruises. The Native Americans he met on his travels considered Johnny Appleseed a great and knowledgeable medicine man who could help them cure their illnesses.

CELEBRATE!

Johnny Appleseed Today

You can become a Johnny Appleseed yourself—all you need is an apple or two, an egg carton, and some potting soil or dirt from your garden.

Tear off the top of the egg carton and fill all the egg cups nearly to the top with the soil. If your carton is plastic or Styrofoam, poke a hole in the bottom of each cup with a pencil point so extra water can drain out, and put the carton on a tray to catch the water. Use a tray under a cardboard carton too, because it will leak a little water.

Water the soil gently until it feels damp all the way to the bottom. Eat your apples and pick out the seeds from the cores. If you have two different kinds of apples, keep their seeds separate so you'll know which are which. Now poke a hole about ½ inch deep in each egg cup with a pencil or your finger and drop a seed into each hole. Cover it carefully with the soil and set the egg carton in a sunny window.

Don't be impatient—your apple seeds will take at least two weeks to sprout. Keep the soil damp but not soaking wet while you're waiting and after the seedlings begin to grow. When they are about two to three inches tall, you can transplant them into larger pots. Your seeds will probably never become trees that bear fruit, but they have beautiful leaves and make pretty potted plants for years.

Conduct a Taste Test

How many kinds of apples do you and your family eat? Most stores in the United States only sell a few varieties, such as red and golden delicious, Rome beauty, Granny Smith, and McIntosh. If you're lucky, you may find Staymans, Cortlands, Macouns, Jonathans, Gravensteins, winesaps, pippins, greenings, or northern spies. And in earlier times there were many more kinds of apples that are nearly unknown today.

Different varieties of apples are grown for different purposes. Some are considered best for eating raw, others best for cooking, and still others mainly useful for cider. Try making a comparison of apple varieties to see which you and your friends like best and for what reasons.

Get two apples each of as many kinds as you can. Set one example of each variety on a table, making a long row. Slice the other apple and set the slices on a dish in front of the whole one. Be sure to label each variety. Now you're ready for your taste test.

You can have as many taste testers as you want, as long

as you have enough slices of each apple for every tester. Agree on the categories you will use to judge the apples and make a list. You might compare flavor (sweet, tart, bland); texture (hard, soft, crisp, mealy, juicy); color of inside flesh (white, yellowish); color of skin (dark or light red, yellow, green); texture of skin (smooth, bumpy, tough, thin); size; shape; or anything else that seems important.

When you're finished, compare your answers. You may find that most of the testers like some apples much better than others. The less-popular varieties may be better for cooking and baking. Now you and your friends will know what to look for when you go to the store. But if you see a kind of apple that's new to you, be sure to give it a try.

March 17

St. Patrick's Day

Patron saint of Ireland, St. Patrick was a real man who was born around A.D. 389 and probably died in 461. The exact dates aren't known and while this holiday to honor him is supposed to be on the day he died, no one is sure about that either. Amazingly enough, St. Patrick wasn't Irish by birth. He was born and raised in England until he was a teenager.

In those days England was part of the Roman Empire. The Romans had converted people to Christianity and taught many of them how to read and write. But the Romans had not conquered Ireland and when Patrick was sixteen, he was captured by raiders from Ireland who took him there and sold him into slavery.

Unlike England and much of the rest of Europe, Ireland was inhabited by small tribes of people who couldn't read or write and who practiced an ancient form of religion under leaders called Druids. Patrick escaped from Ireland, but he vowed to return. He studied in European monasteries and after several years was sent back to Ireland as a bishop. There he spent the rest of his life teaching the people of Ireland to read and write while converting them to Christianity.

Instead of attempting to stamp out ancient rites, Patrick tried to combine old customs with new meanings. Still, his life was in constant danger because there were always people who didn't want change. However, as time went on he was loved more and more. When he died, all of Ireland went into mourning.

During his lifetime Patrick's fame as a teacher and missionary spread throughout the Western world. As the Roman Empire collapsed and Europe was overrun by barbarians, Ireland became a stronghold of learning. It became known as the "Island of Saints and Scholars." During the Dark Ages, when education and the arts had almost disappeared in Europe, St. Patrick's teachings kept learning alive in Ireland. Throughout the centuries after his death, St. Patrick's teachings kept the light of literacy, of reading and writing, burning brightly.

There are many stories of amazing things St. Patrick is supposed to have done. It is said that once he escaped from his enemies by turning himself and his companions into a herd of deer. Another story tells how one of his friends was saved from fire because he was wearing Patrick's robe. The most famous legends are about how Patrick drove all the snakes out of Ireland. Although it is true that there are no snakes native to Ireland, it is unlikely that they're not there because Patrick cast a magic spell.

While the legends about St. Patrick's feats are fun and interesting to hear, the truth about him is what made him a great and famous man. Almost single-handedly he saved the fundamentals of civilization for the Western world. And it is through him that Ireland has its centuries-old tradition of scholarship and literature.

Did You Know . . . ?

Ireland is known as the Emerald Isle because of the lush green color of the landscape. Its mild, moist climate is ideal for vegetation and a type of clover called shamrock grows everywhere. This three-leafed plant has become a symbol of Irish heritage and many people wear green sprigs of shamrock on St. Patrick's Day.

In fact, green is the color everyone associates with St. Patrick's Day; both in the United States and in Ireland, people wear something green on this holiday. At one time, a person who wasn't wearing green on St. Patrick's Day got a little pinch from anyone who caught him or her.

*

Many people in the United States have Irish ancestors. In fact, there are more people of Irish descent in this country than there are in Ireland. More than half the people who fought in the Revolutionary War were of Irish stock and there were more Irish signers of the Declaration of Independence than any other nationality.

No wonder St. Patrick's Day, honoring Ireland's patron saint, is such a big celebration here. Many cities have parades and other festivities and everywhere you go someone has adopted a lyrical Irish accent for the day.

CELEBRATE!

Make a Chill-Chasing Snake

You might not want to have a real snake slithering around your room, but this cute stuffed toy will stay where you put it and guard you against drafts on cold, windy nights. If you have a gap under your bedroom door or a window that doesn't close exactly right, your cuddly St. Patrick's snake will lie across the threshold and keep you from getting chilled.

You'll probably want your St. Patrick's snake to be green to keep the holiday going all year, but you can make it out of fabric any color or print you like. You need fabric a few inches longer than your doorway or windowsill and five or six inches wide. Inexpensive cotton or cotton blend or even felt will be fine, but avoid loosely woven fabrics, and be sure the material you choose is rugged enough to get kicked around.

Since you want your chill-chaser snake to stay in place, you will fill him with pea gravel, clean sand, or clean cat litter.

With the fabric folded in half the long way and inside out, sew across one end and up the long open side. A sewing machine works best, but hand stitching will do fine if you make your stitches tight and close together—you don't want the stuffing to leak out. Turn the fabric snake right side out by using a mop or broom handle to shove the closed end up through the fabric tube.

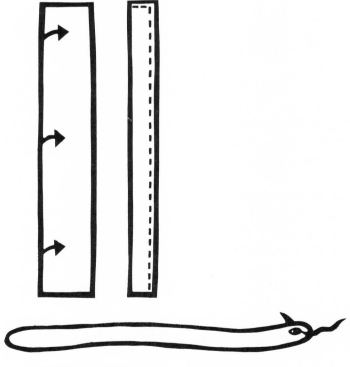

MAKING A CHILL-CHASER SNAKE

Carefully pour in the gravel or sand until the snake is full and fat, then sew the open end closed. Be sure to turn under the raw edges so his lips won't fray. Use fabric marking pens or paint to give your chill-chaser a face and a personality. If you have a scrap of red felt, you can even cut him a tongue and sew that to his lips.

Now you have a pal who will lie across the threshold of your door on chilly nights and keep those drafts from finding you.

Keep Literacy Alive!

This is a project that's fun to do as a class or with a group of your friends. It's appropriate for St. Patrick's Day because it keeps alive his idea of encouraging people to read. And the week of St. Patrick's Day is perfect for your Book Week. Let everybody know that your group is gathering used books that week to be donated to a community center, a preschool, a library, or a hospital.

You can give the books to one place or several. Ask around and see who could make the best use of them. Maybe a local public library, which is always short of funds, needs books for its own collection or holds book sales to raise money. The community day-care center or children's hospital would probably love to have some books for the kids to read. Or maybe your own school library needs assistance.

Make flyers to post at school and on community bulletin boards; encourage everyone to start on spring cleaning early and haul out those favorite books that no one at home reads anymore. Maybe the local paper will run a free ad for you. Be sure to tell people where to deposit the books (you'll want to set up some large, clean boxes as book dumps in handy locations). And let everyone know that you want used children's books that are in good condition, not torn up or scribbled on.

What a thrill you'll all have when you hand over boxes and boxes of books to the places you've decided on. Books are meant to be read and shared and this is an easy way to encourage reading. Be sure to alert the local paper so that someone can cover the story when you make your delivery— this is the kind of news story that makes everyone feel good.

Presenting Spring

Just as fall begins with the autumnal equinox, spring begins with the spring or vernal equinox. On about March 20, day and night are of equal length all over the world. But while fall in the Northern Hemisphere is a time to be thankful for a plentiful harvest, spring is the season for new beginnings. Fields are prepared and seeds are sown for new crops, birds build nests to hold the new eggs, and many animals give birth. In some countries spring marks the beginning of the new year.

Holi

Holi, a spring holiday, is celebrated in March or April by Hindus. It's a favorite day among children, probably because they get to throw or squirt red-colored water on everyone they see that day. Each village has a big bonfire that is considered sacred, and people put ashes from the fire on their foreheads to bring luck in the coming year. Holi is dedicated to Krishna, an incarnation of the god Vishnu.

Passover

An important Jewish holiday, Passover lasts for eight days in late March or early April. It celebrates freedom from slavery, reminding people of the time when Moses led the Israelites out of Egypt. During Passover Jews eat only flat bread called matzoh, because the Israelites left Egypt in such a hurry that there was no time for their bread to rise. On the first two nights of Passover, special dinners called seders are held in Jewish homes. The story of Moses is read, Passover songs are sung, and special foods that symbolize parts of the story are eaten. The table is set with an extra glass of wine; this is for Elijah, the prophet who will return to tell of the Messiah's coming. The wine symbolizes people's hope for peace in the world.

Easter

The most important holiday in the Christian religion is Easter. It is always on a Sunday, the Christians' day of worship, in late March or early April. The date varies because Easter falls on the first Sunday after the first full moon after the spring equinox.

Easter is the day on which Jesus is said to have been raised from the dead after his crucifixion. He thus fulfilled God's promise to send his son to redeem people from sin and save them for all eternity. On Easter, Christians celebrate Jesus' victory over death.

For Christians, Easter is a day of rejoicing. They dress in bright spring colors and go to church to worship, then return home for a family feast. Dyed and decorated eggs have long been part of Easter festivities. Scholars think that Easter eggs symbolize the rebirth of new life in spring and Christ's resurrection in paradise.

Buddhism

There are estimated to be about 303 million Buddhists today, mainly in Asia. Buddhism began with a Hindu prince, Siddhartha Gautama, who lived from about 563 to 483 B.C. in northeastern India. He was born in luxury, but as a young man he went into the world to learn how people could be freed from suffering. One day, after six years of searching, he sat under a *bodhi* tree to meditate. With intense concentration he reached the state of Nirvana, or perfect understanding. Now he was the *Buddha*, the "enlightened one." He spent the rest of his life teaching others how to find enlightenment for themselves.

Buddhism rests on the Four Noble Truths that came to the Buddha in his enlightenment. These Truths are: 1) suffering exists; 2) suffering is caused by desire; 3) suffering can be ended by giving up desire; 4) the Eightfold Path leads to the end of suffering.

The Eightfold Path is really a list of rules for living correctly according to Buddhist beliefs. These rules are: Right Views (accepting the four Noble Truths and the Eightfold Path); Right Resolve (promising yourself to give up all desires and to hurt no living creatures); Right Speech (not telling lies); Right Behavior (not stealing or killing any living creature); Right Occupation (earning your living without harming anyone); Right Effort (trying to get rid of your bad qualities and to acquire good qualities); Right Mindfulness (learning as much as you can about yourself—your body, feelings, and mind); and Right Meditation (following the steps of meditation to reach deeper understanding and enlightenment).

The Buddha believed that each person must find his own path to enlightenment; prayers to the gods or offerings made to priests couldn't help. For the Buddha, nothing in the world was permanent. Everything—objects, people, ideas, the whole world—was always in a state of changing and becoming. The only reality was Nirvana.

In order to search for the Noble Truths and follow the Eightfold Path, a person had to devote his life to meditation. Only someone who was willing to give up home, family, job, and possessions could do it. Such people (almost always men) often became monks who lived the religious life and depended on the rest of the community for their food. Others lived according to Buddhist ideals as much as possible.

Over the centuries, as Buddhism spread through much of Asia, it divided into numerous sects with somewhat differing interpretations of the Buddha's teachings. Each group has monasteries and temples where monks spend their lives following the Eightfold Path in their search for enlightenment.

Buddha's Birthday

Buddhism is a religion that is practiced by each person for himself or herself. There are no major religious holidays that are celebrated as essential parts of the religion. Each temple or community holds local festivals, which often include processions and performances of Buddhist rituals. But there is one holiday that most Buddhists celebrate—Buddha's Birthday.

Actually, since there were no written accounts of the Buddha's life until several centuries after he died, no one can be certain of the exact dates of his birth and death or of the date he achieved enlightenment. Southeast Asia's Buddhists celebrate all three of these events together on a holiday in spring, when lanterns and lights are strung on houses and temples. In some places this holiday is called Wesak and is celebrated in April; in other places it occurs in May.

In Japan Buddha's Birthday is called Flower Day; people decorate special shrines with flowers and pour sweet tea over statues of Buddha as a baby. Buddhists in other countries celebrate this holiday in similar ways.

Buddhist New Year

The new year for Buddhists in many parts of southeast Asia begins in April. The date is decided every year by astrologers. Men playing drums lead a procession to the temple, where people wash the statues of the Buddha; in some places people pour water over one another as well. Perhaps these customs developed because water is so important to life. In Cambodia, new year's games have been played for a thousand years at Angkor, the home of the ancient kings.

April 1

April Fool's Day

The custom of playing April Fool's Day pranks is centuries old. A number of historians think that April Fool's jokes began in the 1500s. At that time the French king decided to adopt the new Gregorian calendar (the one we use today). Before the new calendar, New Year's Day was close to what is now April 1, but the Gregorian calendar changed that holiday to January 1. Maybe the first April fools were the ones who didn't make the adjustment in their calendars! But it's possible that some people pretended to forget to change the date and instead visited friends and brought fake "New Year's" gifts on April Fool's Day.

This is a holiday that encourages practical jokes. The simplest ones are telling people stuff that's not true, like saying "Your shoelaces are untied" and yelling "April fool" when your friend looks down at his shoes. Long ago kids used to glue pennies to the sidewalk and hide to watch people trying to pick them up. Nowadays you'd probably need to glue down a quarter to get anyone to stop and try to retrieve it!

Some April Fool's pranksters would stuff an old purse with wadded paper and tie a piece of fishing line to it. The fishing line was practically invisible and when someone stooped to

123

pick up the purse, the kids would pull on the line and move the purse just a little bit out of reach.

There are lots of classic April Fool's Day jokes that people still play on one another today. Putting salt in the sugar bowl is one and putting hot sauce in someone's drink is another. Anyone who gets a friendly slap on the back from a pal on April Fool's Day has to wonder if at the same time that hand also stuck a sign on his shirt saying "Kick me" or something similar. And on April 1 you don't know if that kind person who tells you there's a smudge on your face is really being helpful or is waiting to see you run to the mirror before yelling "April fool."

It's fun to think up clever April Fool's Day jokes to play on your friends and family. Be careful, though, that things don't get out of hand. Practical jokes can sometimes turn nasty and it's not really in the spirit of this holiday to hurt people's feelings or be mean. Jokes that are really funny or just plain silly will give everyone a good laugh.

Did You Know . . . ?

In Scotland centuries ago one popular April Fool's Day joke was to send a young man to hand deliver an important message. The person who received the message knew the paper had only a silly rhyme on it, but he or she would solemnly refold and seal it and ask the young man to take it on to someone else because it was so important. Thus the "fool" would run all over town on April 1.

*

Some countries celebrate holidays that are similar to April Fool's Day. In Mexico on December 28 you shouldn't lend anything to a friend who asks to borrow it—you'll never get it back. It's expected that anything borrowed on this day will not be returned, and the joke is on the person who forgets what day it is and lends his belongings.

CELEBRATE!

Jokes to Listen To

Make a surprise April Fool's Day gift for Mom or Dad or a friend who likes to listen to tapes: record a riddle-and-joke tape of your own. You can find riddle and joke books in the library if you don't have a whole bunch of them that you know by heart. Borrow a cassette recorder and read or recite the jokes and riddles in a clear voice.

The good thing about tape is that you can rewind it and tape over a joke that just cracked you up so much you could hardly get the words out. After all, it won't be very funny to the listener if all he hears is a bunch of mumbled words and then you laughing while you try to talk.

When you're taping, pause the machine after each joke or riddle and then record a couple of seconds of blank tape, so the person listening has a moment to laugh before you launch into the next one.

And for the April Fool's part of the tape, why not end with a few riddles that you don't give the answers to? Then record the whole riddle and answer on another tape to hand out at the end of the day. You could even hide the second tape in some fairly easy spot and give clues to where it is on the first tape.

Fools in Folk Fiction

Fools, especially fools who end up getting the last laugh, are common figures in folktales all over the world. You may remember some "fool" stories from when you were younger. Tales like "The Three Sillies" and "Noodlehead" are widely known, and so is the story of foolish Epaminondas. There is a whole series of Yiddish stories about the Fools of Chelm. And what about "The Emperor's New Clothes"? Though it's not a folktale, it's definitely a tale of a fool.

Your whole class can have fun making picture books of fool stories. How many different ones can you find? Get the kids in your class to bring in their favorite old books that tell fool stories. Each person should choose a different story for his or her own book. If you need more, or if you want to find some unusual ones that aren't so well known, here's how to look for them in the library.

How to find a fool

First try looking under "Fools" in the card catalog or microfiche. You might discover a whole group of stories done as picture books for little kids. If you don't find much here, however, there's a way to find these stories in collections of folk and fairy tales.

Ask the librarian for the reference book called *Index to Fairy Tales*. Look up the entry for "Fools and foolishness"; it gives a long list of fool stories. Pick out one that sounds interesting; then look up the entry for that story in the main part of the *Index*. For example, if you wanted to know where to find a version of "The Three Sillies," you would look under that title; there are two versions listed, in two different collections of folk and fairy tales. (You have to look in the front of the book to get the full names of these collections.)

Your library won't have every fairy-tale collection referred to in the *Index*, but there will probably be enough for you to find several good fool stories to choose from.

Write it your way

Of course, for the book you will write and illustrate, you won't use the exact words of the story you read in the collection. You'll tell that story in your own words. It's okay to use these stories, however; no one knows who first made most of them up, and they have been told for hundreds of years by different storytellers. Folk and fairy tales are retellings of old and famous stories, and your version will be an interesting addition to the many ways the story has been presented. Details can be changed in any way you like. For instance, you might want to modernize it and set it in the present time in your own hometown.

When you've written the story in your own words, plan your book. Use whole sheets of paper and copy one or two paragraphs of the story on each one. Then use the blank part of the paper for your illustration. Experiment with placing the words and pictures on the top or bottom of each page, or try having a page of words and then a page of only pictures.

You can use staples or yarn to hold your book together, and you can add a cover made of construction paper with the title and your name.

Share the foolishness

When all the books are finished, it's fun to pass them around so everyone can read all of them. You may be surprised at how similar some fool stories are to one another, even when they come from different countries. And you may also be amazed at how terrific all your books look. Maybe you can read your story to your younger brothers and sisters. Or perhaps you can all visit the lower grade classrooms and read the little kids your fool stories on April Fool's Day.

April 2

International Children's Book Day

April 2 is the birthday of Hans Christian Andersen, the famous Danish writer of fairy tales for children. So it's appropriate for International Children's Book Day to be celebrated on this date. The holiday is sponsored by the International Board on Books for Young People (called IBBY). IBBY's purpose is to encourage worldwide understanding and friendship through children's books.

Every year a different country is the official sponsor of International Children's Book Day; every other year IBBY presents Hans Christian Andersen Awards to one author and one illustrator whose work is considered especially important. Some people who have won the Hans Christian Andersen medal in the past are Americans, including Maurice Sendak, Scott O'Dell, Paula Fox, and Virginia Hamilton; others are from Norway, the Netherlands, Australia, and many other countries.

But why is Hans Christian Andersen so important to IBBY and International Children's Book Day? Andersen was born in Denmark in 1805. He wanted to be an actor, but he wasn't making enough money to live on, so at age thirty he began writing fairy tales. People liked the stories so well that he continued to write them for the rest of his life.

Andersen's fairy tales are some of the best-known stories ever written for children. They have been translated into more languages than any book except the Bible and they have been made into plays, movies, and recordings. You have probably read some of Andersen's stories yourself—tales like "The Ugly Duckling," "The Emperor's New Clothes," "The Little Mermaid," "The Steadfast Tin Soldier," and many other much-beloved fairy tales.

Unlike the Brothers Grimm, who wrote down old folktales they heard from people in villages in Germany, Hans Andersen made up his fairy tales. But his stories have proved to be as memorable for children everywhere as those older tales that were passed down as spoken traditions through many generations. Andersen's fairy tales are good examples of children's stories that are known and loved all over the world.

Did You Know . . . ?

Hans Christian Andersen's own life was kind of like a fairy tale. His family was very poor and they lived in a one-room cottage that served as bedroom, kitchen, and shoemaker shop for Hans's father. Then, when Hans was eleven, his father died. Hans had trouble in school and he did not do well in the jobs he tried.

Hans left home when he was fourteen and tried to find work as a singer and actor. With the help of a well-to-do friend, Hans went back to school at age seventeen; the other students made fun of him because he was so much older than they were, and the schoolmaster was very cruel. Still, Hans worked hard and when he was twenty-four he completed his education and began writing books and essays. By the end of his life Hans Christian Andersen was famous all over the world. Like the Ugly Duckling in his story, he turned out very different from what people had expected.

*

Books are important in most kids' lives. When you were little, someone probably read picture books and ABCs with you. Now perhaps you read exciting novels, collections of poetry, or nonfiction books about subjects you're interested in—or all three. But did you know that books written especially for children and young people haven't been around very long? Fairy tales and folktales like those the Brothers Grimm collected were enjoyed by the whole family, not just the children. And many novels that young people like you have read and enjoyed for years, such as *Robinson Crusoe* and *The Three Musketeers*, were written for adults, not children. Books meant for children got started around 1700, but most of them were intended to teach children lessons about the world. It was only in the 1800s that people began writing books for kids that were just meant to be enjoyed. Aren't you glad they did?

CELEBRATE!

The Reading Circle

A perfect way to celebrate International Children's Book Day is to read a book or two to some younger kids. Having the big kids spend time with them is a treat for little ones. And besides, it will give you a chance to reread that story that was your all-time favorite when you were little.

Get a group of friends together and talk with the principal of the elementary school about this project. Maybe you could spend a whole morning going to the kindergarten and first- and second-grade classes. Each of you could gather three or four of the younger kids in a corner of the classroom or in the library. Choose two or three stories that aren't too long so you'll have time to finish them. And be sure to let the children know that you loved these stories when you were their age—they'll feel proud that you're sharing these special books with them.

Another good place to read to kids is the public library. Talk to the librarian to find out when you could do this and what age groups you might read to. You may have so much fun reading to the kids that you'll decide to have a Children's Book Day every week!

What If Characters Could Talk?

Here's a way for your whole class to celebrate International Children's Book Day—and all it takes is paper and pencil and lots of imagination. Think about your favorite character in a book and then try writing a letter from that character.

You can decide as a group who your characters should write to. Perhaps you want to write a letter from your character to yourself as a real person. Or maybe you'd rather have your character write to another character in the same book—or in a different book. For example, if you use Hans Christian Andersen's fairy tales, the Princess from "The Princess and the Pea" could write to the Emperor from "The Emperor's New Clothes." Or maybe a character from a fairy tale, like Cinderella, could write a letter to someone in a book by Judy Blume. Or what if the Ugly Duckling wrote to Wilbur from *Charlotte's Web*—they might have a lot in common.

Before you start your letter, give some thought to what kind of person your character is and what kinds of things he or she would talk about in a letter. It can be funny to imagine what a character from the past would think about things we take for granted—television, cars, airplanes, and computers.

If you get really involved in this project, the characters in your class can have a continuing correspondence through the rest of the year. Put the letters up on the wall or publish them in a booklet so other people can enjoy them too. You might even want to send copies to the publishers of the books the characters appear in so they can see what these characters are up to when they're outside their books!

April 22

Earth Day

The first Earth Day was held on April 22, 1970. By that time many people were becoming worried about the survival of our planet as they watched governments, industries, and individuals pollute our air and water and do other destructive things to our environment.

Ever since the Industrial Revolution, air pollution has been a problem, but concern about it wasn't very widespread. For decades people have thrown trash and litter onto highways and into lakes, streams, and oceans, but not very many people thought it was a big problem. After all, there were always places where the air was clean and fresh. And it seemed that little bits of litter couldn't really amount to much. However, as the world's population grew and consumer demands increased, we all found out that there's a limit to how much our earth can handle.

We started hearing about global warming and deforestation, holes in the ozone layer, and more and more animal species becoming extinct. People began to realize that the earth's resources are limited and that if we use them and destroy them at such a fast pace, pretty soon there won't be anything left. Life as we know it is being threatened.

The message of the first Earth Day in 1970 was "Give Earth

a Chance." As Earth Day is celebrated each year, it reminds people that they are responsible for the condition of the earth and what's going to happen to it in the future. They are often the ones who litter and pollute. Those same people are the ones who elect governments that don't take environmental dangers seriously. They are the ones who support industries that are irresponsible in their use of our precious resources. And we are those people.

Earth Day gives individuals a time to focus on saving our environment. It's a day of picnics and speeches and community cleanups. But one day a year isn't enough. Earth Day is just a starting point for the year-round activity that's needed to make our planet a good place to live.

Did You Know . . . ?

The biggest Earth Day celebration of all time was held on April 22, 1990, in honor of the twentieth anniversary of Earth Day. Huge crowds gathered in many cities to hear music groups and politicians. Unfortunately, these same people who were together to learn about saving the environment left tons of trash and garbage to be cleaned up at the end of the day. It seems they hadn't totally understood the message of Earth Day.

*

Did you know that you can write to a government office called the Environmental Protection Agency (EPA) for information? They will send lots of material on saving the environment; you can use this information in your classroom or at home. Here's how to get it: write to United States Environmental Protection Agency, Office of Public Affairs, 401 M Street SW, Washington, DC 20460. Your state or city may have a similar agency—look in the phone book to find out.

*

Where do our trees go? It takes years to grow a tree but only a minute or two to use one up. Nearly 2 million *tons* of junk mail arrive in American mailboxes every year. If one million of us stopped getting junk mail, each year we could save 1½ million trees. And how about shopping bags? A single twenty-year-old tree can produce only seven hundred paper grocery bags. How many does your family use in a year?

This information and much more can be found in a paperback book called *50 Simple Things You Can Do to Save the Earth* (Earthworks Press, 1989).

*

The plastic rings that hold your soft drink cans together are extremely dangerous to sea animals and birds. Since the plastic is so hard to see in the water, baby animals like seals and sea lions get the rings caught around their necks. Then as they grow larger, the animals are strangled. Pelicans who get their bills trapped in these rings can't open their mouths to eat, and they starve.

You can help in a very easy way. Always clip the rings of six-pack holders with scissors before throwing them away. And of course you should never toss them in the water or on the beach—put them in a garbage bin.

CELEBRATE!

Get the Recycling Spirit

How committed are your school and your community to keeping the spirit of Earth Day alive all year long? Many schools and communities still don't have recycling programs. If your school doesn't have one, why don't you and your friends get the ball rolling?

Talk it up

The first thing to do is start talking about how important a recycling program is. Talk up this idea at home too. Your parents pay for your education, through taxes to public schools and perhaps fees to private schools. School officials listen to the people who pay the bills.

You'll also need to get support for a recycling program

from your classmates and teachers. School officials need to feel that the students and teachers want such a program and will work to keep it going.

Recycling at school

The program itself is pretty easy to start. As soon as school leaders get behind the idea, all that's needed are some extra trash cans—for glass, cans, and whatever else your community can recycle—where there used to be just one for trash. Once the marked containers are installed, it's your job to keep reminding people to use them. Some institutions even have a box for used plastic utensils that can be recycled.

Paper too is a trash item that can be separated and recycled. Collection bins for newspapers and office papers will keep them apart from other paper trash. In some communities there is a recycling program for junk mail. After you get this going at school, you can probably have the PTA encourage parents to bring in their papers too and help save some trees.

Recycling at the supermarket

Many markets now have bins where people can bring in those zillions of plastic bags that they get their fruit and vegetables in. And some supermarkets give a few pennies off the food bill for every paper or plastic shopping bag the shopper brings in because then they don't need to use a new one. If the market your parents shop in doesn't have such a program, ask the management to start one. And if a competing market does and yours doesn't, point that out to the manager. Shoppers are becoming increasingly aware of how much packaging and other paper and plastic stuff they get and have to throw away.

Recycling in your community

What is your community doing about recycling? Is there a separate pickup for newspapers? What about cans and bot-

COLLECTION OF RECYCLED ITEMS

tles? Make a class project of writing letters to the editor of your local paper and to the mayor. Local government officials usually will respond to citizens' concerns. After all, your parents can vote now and you will be able to before long.

Another Method of Recycling

Besides putting stuff in separate trash containers so that it can be reprocessed, why not recycle things at home by creating new uses for them? This can be something extremely simple. For example, the plastic tops to coffee cans are great "coasters" for drippy bottles of detergent or salad dressing; they're also perfect for holding soppy sponges and scouring pads or even as free soap dishes at the kitchen sink.

But you can easily and inexpensively make real coasters for glasses and mugs out of those round plastic lids. Just cut out circles of felt or blotting paper to fit the insides of the coffee-can lids and glue them in place with white glue. Besides being really cheap to make, these coasters have another great feature—they're big enough to hold even the oversized mug Mom uses for her morning coffee or a big bottle of soda pop.

Other items that are easily and cheaply converted from trash to useful objects are gallon plastic milk containers and various metal food cans. If you cut off the top third of a gallon milk container, the bottom makes a terrific leak-proof holder for a large potted plant. Or you can use it as a small toy box—just the thing to hold all your little sister's crayons, Lego pieces, or doll clothes.

See Father's Day (page 160) for ideas on how to recycle tuna and vegetable cans into desk accessories or handyman holdalls. Or why not give yourself a present? Clean and decorate a tuna can to make a rubber-band or paper-clip holder; do the same with a vegetable can to create a pencil holder. When you make these useful items, you're giving the earth a present at the same time.

May 1

Mother Goose Day

Mother Goose Day was created as a special time to stop and think about those traditional rhymes we all loved when we were little. The motto of this celebration is "Either alone or in sharing, read childhood nursery favorites and feel the warmth of Mother Goose's embrace."

Most people can remember lots of nursery rhymes once they get started. You can probably provide the rest of the verses that begin "Jack be nimble, Jack be quick" or "Little Boy Blue, come blow your horn" or "Hickory dickory dock." But why are these rhymes that almost everyone knows called "Mother Goose" rhymes? And who was Mother Goose anyway?

The answer is that no one really knows. Some people think that she was Emperor Charlemagne's mother, Queen Bertha, who was known as "Goose-Footed Bertha." Charlemagne ruled over part of Europe, including what is now France and Germany. Queen Bertha died quite a long time ago, in the year 783; later French legends about an old woman who sat spinning yarn and telling stories to children were supposedly about Goose-Footed Bertha, but no one can be certain.

It does seem, though, that Mother Goose got her start in

138

France in some way. A French book published in 1650 refers to a story that is *"Comme un conte de la Mère Oye"* ("Like a Mother Goose story"); this seems to suggest that *"la Mère Oye"* was already known as a storyteller. And in 1697 Charles Perrault published a book of nursery tales, including "Little Red Riding Hood," "Cinderella," and "Sleeping Beauty." His book was called *Les Contes de Ma Mère l'Oye*, which means *Stories of My Mother Goose*. Perrault's tales were translated into English, and Mother Goose was on her way to fame.

Still later, around 1719, a woman named Elizabeth Goose who lived in Boston helped lull her grandchildren to sleep by reciting rhymes and singing songs. Her son-in-law, a printer, supposedly published these rhymes in a little book called *Songs for the Nursery, or Mother Goose's Melodies*. However, no one has ever found a copy of this book, so perhaps this is only a legend based on the odd name of "Goose."

But however she began, Mother Goose is definitely here to stay. New collections of Mother Goose rhymes are published frequently, and parents keep their own older copies to hand down to their children and grandchildren. The rhymes, some of them very ancient, have lasted through many generations of children. There must be something especially pleasing to children's ears about these nonsense verses. Try reciting some of your own favorites right now—your friends will probably join in, because Mother Goose's rhymes are almost impossible to forget.

Did You Know . . . ?

There are lots of theories about the origins of many well-known Mother Goose rhymes. For example, here is

> *Mistress Mary, quite contrary,*
> *How does your garden grow?*
> *With silver bells and cockleshells*
> *And pretty maids all in a row.*

Many people think that "Mistress Mary" was Mary, Queen of Scots, who lived from 1542 to 1587. She had four ladies-in-waiting, all named Mary (Mary Beaton, Mary Seaton, Mary Fleming, and Mary Livingston), and of course these are the "pretty maids all in a row." Queen Mary liked music ("silver bells") and some scholars claim that "cockleshells" decorated one of her favorite dresses.

Lots of other real people appear in Mother Goose rhymes. Old King Cole was a British king in the third century; he was much loved by his subjects and he was supposedly very fond of music, which is probably why he "called for his fiddlers three." Little Jack Horner is believed to have been a man named Thomas Horner who lived in the sixteenth century. At that time King Henry VIII of England was confiscating property that belonged to churches. Thomas Horner carried a Christmas present to the king—a pie that contained the deeds to twelve large estates. On the way he stopped and took out one of the deeds for himself. It must have been a very strange pie, but it certainly provided a nice "plum" for Mr. Horner!

While lots of other rhymes refer to real people and historical events, however, some Mother Goose verses are simply nonsense.

*

Not everyone loves nursery rhymes. Over the years many people have objected to Mother Goose because they felt the verses mentioned things that weren't good for children to hear or think about. One man went so far as to count the bad things that happen in a typical collection of Mother Goose rhymes. He listed "2 cases of choking to death, 1 case of death by devouring, 1 case of cutting a human being in half," and on and on—he found more than 150 "unsavoury" incidents.

But most people realize that these examples of death and injury aren't meant to be taken seriously. Little children don't seem to worry much about them—they know that these rhymes are just for fun. Mother Goose's bad boys and naughty girls are there to be laughed at, not to be cried over.

CELEBRATE!

A Game of Mother Goose

Since Mother Goose rhymes appeal mainly to young children, why not celebrate Mother Goose Day with a bunch of little kids? Of course you can read the rhymes to them or recite your favorites aloud with the kids—they probably know most of them by heart. But when you're tired of reading, here's a Mother Goose game you can make to play with young children.

Your game will be designed generally on the same idea as Candyland. To make it, you need a piece of stiff cardboard for the game board and paints or felt pens to color it in. Make a winding path that starts at one corner of the board and ends up in the opposite corner, twisting and doubling back to use as much space as you like. Draw lines to divide the pathway into sections for each player's game piece to move along. Game pieces can be small toys or cutout colored cardboard circles. You'll also need a die to throw; this will determine how many spaces on the path each player moves on each turn.

Now comes the fun part. Think about some of your own favorite nursery rhymes and adapt their characters and events to your game. For example, a player might land on a space that's under Little Boy Blue's haystack; that player loses a turn because, like Little Boy Blue, he is "fast asleep." Or perhaps a player lands on Little Miss Muffet's tuffet; that player too loses a turn because Little Miss Muffet got "frightened away."

On the other hand, you might include a space for the cow who jumped over the moon; a player who lands there might get to jump ahead four or five spaces. A space for the black sheep might allow a player to go ahead three spaces, one for each of the three bags of wool.

Your own imagination will give you plenty of ideas for other Mother Goose rhymes that can be worked into your game. You can draw pictures of the characters alongside the path. You might make a rule that a player has to recite the appropriate rhyme when he or she lands on a space that involves that rhyme. Try out other variations that will make your game more fun. After you've played it a few times, you might want to make some changes in it, based on what works well and what doesn't as you play.

Now gather up some little kids and have fun teaching them to play your Mother Goose game.

Create Mother Goose Land

Here's an opportunity to let your imagination take over and create a sculptured drawing of a scene from one of Mother Goose's rhymes. You could choose Little Boy Blue's haystack in the field or the Old Woman's shoe or whatever setting you like best. And don't worry if you're not the best artist in the world—you don't need to be skillful to make a sculptured drawing that's interesting and unusual.

You need white glue, a pencil, plain white uncooked rice, and brightly colored construction paper. Choose a color that evokes the feeling of the rhyme: yellow usually looks cheerful, while orange might look angry.

Draw the scene lightly in pencil on the construction paper; keep it simple, without too many intricate details. Once you're happy with it, it's time to apply the glue. You can draw with the glue nozzle over the pencil outlines, or you can spread glue with a small piece of paper towel to fill in some of the shapes. Don't spread the glue too thin or the rice won't stick to it.

When the glue is applied where you want it, sprinkle the rice over the whole paper. Let it sit for a while until the glue dries. Then hold the paper over a wastebasket and let the extra, non-glued rice slide off. You'll be amazed at how terrific your drawing looks with its simple shapes and color scheme and its pebbly texture created by the rice.

You can experiment with other 3-D effects in your pictures. Try using uncooked pasta, such as elbow macaroni, to make hats or arms and legs; use toothpicks to create roads and houses. Buttons, cotton balls, and small bits of ribbon and fabric are other possibilities, and you'll probably come up with lots more as you proceed. Just be careful that the objects you use aren't too heavy to stay glued to the paper.

Display the sculptured drawings when they're finished; write the first line of each one's rhyme under it so viewers can pick out their old-time favorites.

May, second Sunday

Mother's Day

Mother's Day is a happy celebration, a time when people remember their mothers and express their appreciation for everything their mothers have done for them. It's a day for doing little things that show your love and respect for a very important woman in your life.

The custom of honoring mothers is centuries old. In England as far back as the 1600s, there was a day called "Mothering Sunday" that was celebrated on the fourth Sunday of Lent (Lent is the forty-day period before Easter). Many poor people in England worked as servants for wealthier folk; they lived in the houses where they worked and almost never got any time off. Usually they had traveled far from their own homes to find work, and so they didn't see their families very often. But on Mothering Sunday servants got a day off and were encouraged to go home and spend a day with their mothers. Often they took along a special cake called a "mothering cake" to provide a festive meal.

Mother's Day as it is celebrated in the United States was first suggested in 1872 by Julia Ward Howe, the woman who wrote the words to the "Battle Hymn of the Republic." She hoped it would become a day dedicated to peace, and she organized Mother's Day meetings in Boston for several years. Other people too began celebrating Mother's Day in their own communities, but the idea didn't really catch on until 1907.

In that year a woman named Anna Jarvis who lived in Philadelphia started a campaign to establish a national Mother's Day. Anna's own mother had wanted to find ways to heal the wounds left by the Civil War and had hoped that mothers would bring their children together in peace. Anna Jarvis asked her mother's church in Grafton, West Virginia, to hold a Mother's Day celebration on the second Sunday in May, the second anniversary of her mother's death.

The following year, 1908, there were Mother's Day celebrations in Grafton and in Philadelphia. Anna Jarvis talked to lots of people and got them to write letters to ministers, politicians, and businessmen to support the idea of Mother's Day. By 1911 Mother's Day was celebrated in almost every state. In 1914 President Woodrow Wilson made an official announcement proclaiming the second Sunday in May as Mother's Day, and that's when it has been ever since.

In many other places, such as Denmark, Finland, Italy, Turkey, Australia, and Belgium, Mother's Day is celebrated on the second Sunday in May. Different dates are set for a similar holiday in other countries. But whenever it's observed, Mother's Day is a fine time to let your mother know how much you love her.

Did You Know . . . ?

The idea of a mother as a being who gives life to her children and who protects and nourishes them until they can care for themselves is a very powerful symbol. Many people believe that Mother's Day grew out of much older celebrations that were held in the spring to honor Rhea, the Mother of the Gods, in ancient Greece and Asia Minor. Later, as Christianity spread through Europe, this festival was modified to

honor the "Mother Church," which for Christians represented the spiritual power that gave them life and protected
them from harm. At some time this church festival became
linked to the idea of Mothering Sunday, when people honored
their own mothers as well as their church.

*

Carnations are the flowers that belong to Mother's Day. Perhaps this is because in the "language of flowers" carnations
stand for sweetness, purity, and endurance—qualities that
people might associate with mothers. However, the real reason may be that carnations were Anna Jarvis's mother's favorite flowers. Bouquets of carnations were used in the first
Mother's Day church services in 1907 and 1908, and soon it
became the custom to wear a carnation on Mother's Day.

CELEBRATE!

Give Mom a Day Off

Most mothers think that the very best way to celebrate Mother's Day is for them to relax and take it easy all day while
the rest of the family does the work. And giving Mom breakfast in bed is a great way to start things off.

The day before Mother's Day, have a conference with your
dad, your brothers and sisters, and whoever else will be involved. Decide what you're going to give Mom for breakfast,
so you'll have time to buy anything that's needed. Mother's
Day breakfast doesn't have to be fancy or elaborate; juice,
coffee or tea, and a muffin or croissant might be just what
your mom needs to be perfectly happy. But you'll want to
make sure you have it all together in advance.

On Mother's Day let Mom sleep a little late while the rest
of you get things ready very quietly. If possible, make the
tray look fancy with a pretty mat and napkin and maybe a
couple of flowers in a little vase. If your mother likes to read
the Sunday papers, bring them in along with the breakfast
tray. Put the Mother's Day cards on the tray too, so she can
open them while she's sipping her juice.

Don't forget that Mother's Day lasts all day! Your mother shouldn't have to take her tray back to the kitchen or wash her dishes. You and the rest of the family should plan to do every chore today, from walking the dog to getting stuff ready for school the next morning. Some mothers find it hard to sit still and do nothing around the house for a whole day, but after a while they get used to it! And your mother will definitely appreciate the chance to sit back and realize what a wonderful family she has.

Picture This for Mother's Day

A perfect gift for your mom on Mother's Day is a picture of you in a pretty frame. Each child in the family can make his or her own frame with a photo in it. Or, if you have a good picture of all the kids together, you might want to make a frame for that photo. (If you don't have any photos you like, why not draw a picture of yourself? Even if it's not a perfect likeness, Mom will love it.)

The size of your frame depends on the size of the photo you're using. Lay the photo flat on a sheet of plain white paper and draw around it for the size. Then decide if the frame should come in a little closer around the edge to cover up the white border of the photo; also decide how wide you want your frame to be. Use a ruler to draw a rectangular frame on the paper.

Cut out this paper frame and use it as a pattern to draw your frame on cardboard; the kind that comes on the back of a pad of writing paper is about the right weight. Cut out the cardboard frame carefully.

Now you can decide how to decorate it. You can use colored felt pens or crayons or paints to make a design; you might prefer to glue pretty wrapping paper onto the cardboard for your frame; you could even wind narrow ribbon around it in an attractive pattern (use tape to hold the ribbon in place).

When the frame is ready, make a backing for it out of cardboard cut to the same size as the frame. Position the

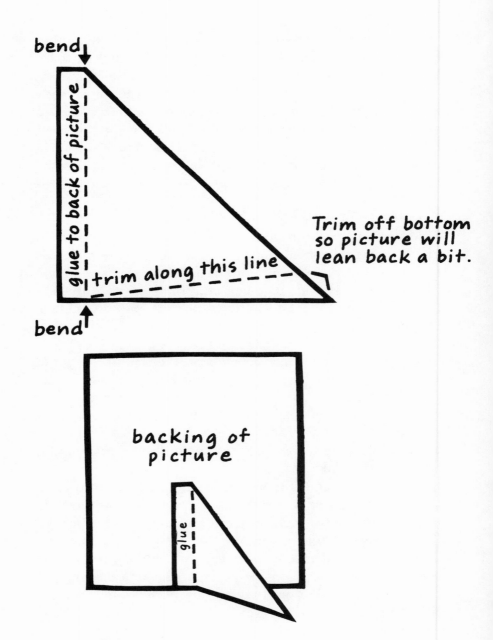

MAKING A PHOTO FRAME AND SUPPORT

photo on top of the backing and under the frame; use short pieces of tape across the photo's corners to keep it from slipping. Then use tape or glue to attach the backing to the frame.

To make your frame stand up, you can attach a support to the back. On the same kind of cardboard you used for the backing, draw a triangle with a narrow rectangle attached to one side. Cut it out; then bend the rectangle part back. Glue this rectangle section to the center of the picture's backing. If the photo doesn't lean back far enough on the support, carefully trim a little off the lower edge of the triangle.

Now you're all ready to wrap your framed picture and give it to your mom on Mother's Day.

May, last Monday

Memorial Day

What does Memorial Day mean besides a day off from school? Did you ever wonder who or what this holiday is a memorial to?

After the Civil War ended in 1865, the people of the United States felt shocked and saddened. The only war ever fought by Americans against one another had left more than 200,000 soldiers dead. Those who came home, and many people who had waited anxiously for the war to end, thought there should be a way to honor the men who had died.

In Columbus, Mississippi, in April 1866, four women went to Friendship Cemetery to decorate the graves of Confederate soldiers. Forty northern soldiers were buried there too, and the women put flowers on these graves of their recent enemies. Their action was publicized in newspapers all over the country.

Around the same time, a druggist named Henry C. Welles in Waterloo, New York, decided his town should hold a celebration to honor the soldiers—both those who had come home and those who had died. He organized a parade of veterans and townspeople to the cemetery, where they dec-

150

orated the soldiers' graves with flags and flowers. They called the holiday Decoration Day; the name was later changed to Memorial Day.

Another person who liked the idea of Decoration Day was General John Logan. He was the head of the Grand Army of the Republic, an organization composed of Union veterans of the Civil War. He said the members of the G.A.R. should decorate the graves of Union soldiers every year on May 30 (the date was changed to the last Monday in May in 1971).

By 1868 the G.A.R. had convinced the government to adopt Decoration Day as a holiday. In the northern states people in nearly every town held a parade to honor the veterans and decorated the soldiers' graves with flags and flowers. The flag in each town was flown at half-mast; patriotic songs were sung, speeches were made, and prayers were offered for peace. Some southern states observed the holiday on the same date, while others honored their dead on different dates.

Memorial Day began as a tribute to those who had died in the Civil War. But as the United States lost soldiers in later wars, those war dead were included in the ceremonies. Today Memorial Day is a time to remember not only those who have died in wars. People decorate their family graves as well. Since 1950 the President's proclamation each year calls Memorial Day a "day of prayer for permanent peace."

Did You Know . . . ?

Decoration Day was a good name for a holiday that honored fallen soldiers. It meant that people decorated their graves, but it also referred to another meaning of "decoration"—a badge of honor or a military award for personal heroism or gallantry. Decorations have been awarded to brave soldiers for centuries; the ancient Greeks and Romans crowned returning soldiers with laurel wreaths to honor their courage.

*

Setting aside a special day to remember and honor the dead is a custom in almost every culture in the world. For example, in Japan the Festival of Lanterns is a day to clean and decorate one's ancestors' graves. In much of Christian Europe the dead are honored on All Souls' Day (November 2). The Zuni of the American Southwest remember their dead on a day whose name can be translated as All Souls' Day. But Memorial Day in the United States is not associated with any particular religion and it holds meaning for all Americans.

*

The women who decorated both Confederate and Union graves in Mississippi so soon after the Civil War's end inspired other people. A lawyer in New York, Francis Miles Finch, described their generosity of spirit and wrote a poem about them called "The Blue and the Gray" (Union soldiers wore blue uniforms, Confederates wore gray). Here is the last verse of his poem.

> *No more shall the war-cry sever,*
> *Or the winding rivers be red:*
> *They banish our anger forever*
> *When they laurel the graves of our dead!*
> *Under the sod and the dew,*
> *Waiting the Judgment Day:—*
> *Love and tears for the Blue;*
> *Tears and love for the Gray.*

CELEBRATE!

A Family Memory Book

Perhaps you've never known a family member who has died. No matter how big or small your family is, though, there are people—grandparents, great-grandparents, maybe aunts or uncles—who are no longer alive. Remembering these people is important. It's natural for you to want to know about the family you belong to. And for older members of your family, it means a lot to know that the people they were close to are not forgotten. Memorial Day is the perfect time to start a family memory book.

Use a loose-leaf notebook for your memory book. That way it's easy to add new pages wherever you need them. You'll need regular lined notebook paper to write on and heavier paper, such as construction paper or notebook dividers, to glue photographs to.

Think about close relatives you know of who have died. Perhaps one or more of your grandparents is no longer alive. Or maybe a cousin or a brother or sister was killed in an accident or was the victim of disease. If you're one of the lucky people whose whole immediate family is still living, your grandparents will remember their own parents and their brothers and sisters who would have been your great-uncles and great-aunts.

You will make a page of your book for each person in your family who has died. For each one, write down the facts at the top of the page: their names, when they were born and when they died, the names of their husbands and wives and of their children if they had any. Be sure to note also how they were related to you: you might write "Uncle Richard was my mom's brother."

If you knew the person, write down your memories of him or her. You might say that when you were really little, Grandpa scared you with his deep voice and bushy whiskers, but as you got older, you loved spending time with him working on his stamp collection.

If the person died before you were born, now is your chance to learn more about your family. Ask an older family member—maybe your grandmother or your dad—to tell you about that person; write down the important memories they describe. It might be the way the person looked or his habit of playing practical jokes or her love of cats and dogs. You don't have to tell everything. The idea is to capture the things that made that person special. You may even decide to add a page for your family's dog who was your best friend when you were little.

If you have photographs of the person you're writing about, choose a few and glue them to the divider page. Be sure to note when and where each photo was taken, if possible.

You might feel awkward asking questions about someone who died. But don't be surprised if you end up spending an hour hearing all about Uncle Jim's antique cars or Grandma Smith's journey across the United States to meet Grandpa. People like to know that the ones they loved will not be forgotten, and they want to share their memories with you.

Your book won't be finished in one day, and in years to come you will probably add new names to it. Each Memorial Day might be a good time to look at your book and add pages for any family members who have died during the year.

Your Family Memory Book is yours to keep and add to, but it would also make a wonderful gift for relatives. It's easy to make photocopies of the pages of your book; put them in their own binder and be sure to put a title and a date on each one. Family members will be delighted that you want to share your memories of the people they loved.

Songs to Remember

Wars have inspired some of the best-known songs in every language. For soldiers, alone and afraid, songs helped lift their spirits and reminded them of home. And for their families, popular songs gave hope that the war would soon be over. In the days before radio made the top tunes available to everyone wherever they were, soldiers made music for themselves. Their songs bound them together and made them feel less alone.

Some soldier songs of Civil War times are still well known today, such as "Battle Hymn of the Republic" and "Tenting Tonight on the Old Camp Ground." Another song, "When Johnny Comes Marching Home," expresses everyone's hope that the soldiers would return safely from the battlefield. Learning songs like these is a great way to explore history; it gives you an idea of what ordinary people felt as momentous events happened around them.

It's easy to find the words and music for songs from the Civil War and for later ones as well. Libraries have collections of song books, and many of them are arranged by topic or by the date when they were written. But once you've found the songs, what can you do with them?

Why not get a group of friends together and practice singing some of these wonderful old songs? You could perform them at a school assembly, but it might be more fun to give an informal concert at a local retirement home. Older people, who may be too ill or frail to get out much, don't have many chances to see live performances or to meet new people. They love to be around young people, but kids often feel uncomfortable because they don't know what to say. A songfest gives you something to do, and you may be surprised at how many of the older folks sing along with you.

Ask your teacher or a parent to call the home's director and arrange a time for your group to go there. Then make photocopies of the words to the songs so everyone will be able to join in. See if there is a piano available; it's not essential, but if one of your group or a resident of the home can play as you sing, it adds to the fun. Don't feel you have to limit your Memorial Day songfest to Civil War songs; look up some songs from later wars too. "Over There" from World War I is a song many older people will know, even if they weren't alive during that war. And maybe they'll teach you some terrific songs you've never even heard of.

Performing songs that recall our nation's history gives you a link to the past we all share and a bridge across the generations. It's a great way to celebrate Memorial Day.

June 14

Flag Day

Since ancient times, flags have been used for many reasons. Usually a flag is a rectangular piece of fabric with a distinctive design; it can be a signaling device or a symbol for a nation. A ship's flag indicates the country where the ship is registered; an army's flag lets everyone know which side the soldiers are fighting for.

When European explorers claimed land for their kings and queens, they planted their country's flag to show who now owned this new territory. Modern explorers plant their country's flag to show who got there first. When Robert Peary became the first person to reach the North Pole in 1909, he marked the spot with an American flag. And, of course, our stars and stripes have been on the moon since Apollo 11 landed there in 1969.

But where did our flag come from? On June 14, 1777, the Second Continental Congress adopted a design for an American flag; "Resolved: that the flag of the United States be thirteen stripes, alternate red and white; that the union be thirteen stars, white in a blue field, representing a new constellation." They planned to add a new star and a new stripe every time a state came into the union. By 1792 there were fifteen stars and fifteen stripes.

Congress didn't realize at first how many states there would be. But by 1818 they could tell that this idea would result in a very long flag. So they decided to limit the number of stripes to thirteen for the original thirteen states and add a new star for each new state. And this plan is still in effect.

Flag Day commemorates the date the official design of the American flag was adopted by the Second Continental Congress. While it's not a national legal holiday, many families display an American flag to observe it. Of course, government buildings display our nation's flag every business day. But did you notice that they often fly a state flag as well?

Each state has its own flag with its own design. In fact, cities and many government officials, such as the president, the secretary of state, the postmaster general, the secretaries of the Army, Navy, and Air Force, as well as the Marine Corps and the Coast Guard, all have their own flags. The designs of these flags all have symbolic meaning; for instance, the secretary of the Navy's flag has an anchor and the secretary of the interior's flag has a buffalo in the middle of it.

The American flag is a symbol of our nation and of people's feelings of patriotism. Flag Day is a good time to think about what it means to be an American.

Did You Know . . . ?

People have long believed that Betsy Ross made the first American flag with her own hands after the design had been adopted. No one knows for sure whether this is true, but certainly someone in Philadelphia made it. At the Betsy Ross House in Philadelphia, they don't have any doubts. Every year on Flag Day there is a program followed by a band concert in the garden, and Betsy Ross is a familiar figure in Fourth of July parades.

*

Did you know that before the official design was adopted, there were lots of other colonial flags? Several of them have a design that includes a rattlesnake and the words "Don't tread on me." Rattlesnakes are found only in the Americas and the colonists must have thought of them as creatures that were well equipped to defend themselves when they were threatened. These flags made a statement: "Don't mess with us or you'll get hurt."

*

Most people believe that our country's flag should be treated with respect, and there are certain customs that are followed when the flag is flown. The American flag must never be "dipped" (lowered slightly) to any object or person (such as a king) while being carried in a parade. On a flagpole, it should be raised quickly but lowered slowly and ceremoniously. The American flag should never be allowed to touch the ground. When it is lowered at sunset, it is often folded in a "military fold." For a military fold, the flag is first folded lengthwise in half and then in half again; then it is folded in a series of triangles starting from the stripe end.

CELEBRATE!

Send a Flag to a Friend

It's interesting to look at the symbols that are used on state flags and early colonial flags and to try to guess what they mean. Some of them are quite beautiful, while others are a little strange. A big dictionary, such as the one in a library, or an almanac usually has a page of color pictures of many kinds of flags. You can use these pictures as models for making postcards.

Buy plain postcards from the post office and make them into flag picture postcards. On the stamped side draw a line down the middle to divide it into a space for your message and a space for the address. On the blank side, copy the design of a flag you think is interesting. (If possible, use some kind of waterproof color so if the postcard gets wet before it's delivered, your flag won't run.)

You could make a whole set of cards to give to someone

or to keep and send to friends yourself. What about doing a set of all the states' flags or a series of historical American flags? Or what about a set of all the flags of the countries of South America or Europe? Military flags, government flags, even signal flags that semaphore operators use are other possibilities. Be sure to label each one so the person you send it to will know what it is.

A set of flag postcards makes a great gift or an unusual and interesting kind of "stationery" for yourself.

Be a Flag Designer

Now that you know that the colors and designs of flags often have symbolic meanings, try designing your own flag. You could make one for your family, for your class or your school, for a club or team you belong to, or just for yourself.

For example, what symbols would represent your family? Two large stars might stand for your parents and a group of smaller stars could be the children, or you might prefer big trees and little acorns. You might use red, white, and blue to show you are Americans, or green and red to indicate that you live on an apple farm. You could divide the flag in half to show the two sides of your family or in thirds to show three generations. Whatever you feel is most important about your family can be symbolized in an imaginative way.

Ask other members of your family for their ideas. When you're happy with your design, you can draw it on a large piece of white paper and put it up for everyone to admire. Perhaps you can organize a family project to sew a family flag out of fabric. Then you can fly it outside in good weather.

If you design a flag for your class or your school, ask if you can make a large one to put up in the school lobby. Other students can help with the project, and maybe other classes will decide to design flags too. A flag makes any group special and gives it a symbol to rally around. Who knows, maybe next year your school will hold a Flag Day parade!

June, third Sunday

Father's Day

Father's Day, as almost everyone knows, is a day to honor Dad. It isn't just for real dads but for any man who acts as a father figure. Stepfathers, uncles, grandfathers, and adult male friends will be delighted to know you appreciate them and their help to you.

Father's Day has been observed in the United States for many years. The first one was on June 19, 1910, in Spokane, Washington. A woman named Mrs. John B. Dodd had requested the holiday to honor fathers and it was made official by the mayor of Spokane and the governor of the state of Washington. Later President Calvin Coolidge supported the idea of this holiday in 1924, but it wasn't presidentially proclaimed an official U.S. holiday until 1966.

Some people felt that adding yet another official holiday only helped greeting card manufacturers. They said that it was dumb for kids to use the money their dads gave them as an allowance to buy a Father's Day card or gift. But that wasn't what Mrs. Dodd had in mind. After all, there weren't any Father's Day greeting cards when she first got the holiday going. She probably just wanted a special day when kids and adults would remember to say thanks to the dads who helped

160

them all year long. It's easy to forget to tell someone that he's special to you and doing a great job being a dad when you see him all the time. Now fathers can count on at least one day a year when they'll get a little appreciation.

Did You Know . . . ?

Mrs. Dodd had a special reason to express appreciation to her father, William Smart. His wife (Mrs. Dodd's mother) had died giving birth to her sixth child, and Mr. Smart was left with a newborn baby and five other young children to raise all by himself. They lived on a farm in eastern Washington, and when Mrs. Dodd grew up, she realized what a heroic job her father had done.

*

It's amazing how often a new idea occurs to people in different places at about the same time. This happened with the idea for Father's Day. There was a Father's Day celebration in West Virginia in 1908; Mrs. Dodd suggested it in Washington in 1909; in 1911 the idea came up in Chicago and in 1912 in Vancouver, Washington. It's hard to remember that in those days, people couldn't just turn on the television and find out what was happening all over the country. Communication was much more limited than it is now, and probably none of these people knew about the other Father's Day celebrations. It just goes to show that it was a good idea.

CELEBRATE!

Spell It Out for Dad

One way you can show your dad that he's special to you is to make your own Father's Day card. Use a piece of construction paper in one of your dad's favorite colors. Down the left side, write the letters for whatever you call your dad— FATHER, DAD, DADDY—or his first name. You are going to print in an adjective or phrase that starts with each letter, so you'll probably want to practice on plain paper first and make sure you know what you want to say and how to spell it. For instance, if you print FATHER in big letters down the left side, you could add "antastic" after the F, "great dad" after A, "he Best" after T, "umorous" after H, "xtraordinary" after E, and "eally Terrific" after R. Once you start thinking about it, you'll come up with lots of words that will perfectly express how you feel about your dad.

Be sure to add "Happy Father's Day" and your name at the bottom of your card. Then you can leave it at his place on the breakfast table or surprise him with it later in the day.

Get Dad Organized

Whether your dad is a handyman type or a man who spends all his time at a desk, here is a present you can make yourself that's sure to be useful and appreciated—a tool or desk set.

You'll need to think about this project ahead of time and collect containers that will be the right size for the stuff you think your dad will want to put in them. For a workbench, a couple of coffee cans will be just right for screwdriver sets— one for regular head and one for Phillips head screwdrivers. Maybe the bottom of an egg carton will be perfect to separate those tiny screws, nails, and washers that your dad keeps hanging on to. Some fat fruit cans will hold wrenches, and maybe you'll need another coffee can for pairs of pliers. Look around at the tools your dad probably has jumbled together and see what size containers you need.

For a desk set you can use a tuna or cat-food can for paper clips and a vegetable can for pens and pencils. Maybe you'll be able to find a small box with a lid, such as a jewelry box, for stamps. And how about a coffee can for his ruler and letter opener and scissors?

Once you've gathered your containers, make sure they're clean and have no jagged edges. Cans should be washed out with soapy water and thoroughly dried. Take off the paper first.

COLLECTION OF RECYCLED ITEMS

There are a number of ways you can decorate your containers to make them into a set. Sticky-backed paper in an attractive design makes a great covering for the outsides of cans. Or you might want to paint everything (ask at the hardware or paint store for suggestions on what to use) and add comical or fancy stickers. Or get plain-colored sticky-backed paper and cut it into stripes or other designs yourself and stick them on in a pattern.

However you decorate it, this useful set will tell your dad that you cared enough to spend time and thought on his gift from you.

Presenting Summer

For most people summer is the best time of the year. In the Northern Hemisphere, it starts about June 21, which is the summer solstice, the day when there are the most hours of daylight. Warm weather and long days mean kids can play outside more often in summer, and adults come home from work while the sun is still shining.

At the time of the summer solstice, the sun is directly overhead at noon at the Tropic of Cancer. This latitude line is 23½ degrees north of the Equator. So the northern part of the earth gets more sunshine during our spring and summer than the Southern Hemisphere does. Don't forget, though, that at the winter solstice the sun is overhead in the Southern Hemisphere, so the warmest months in Australia or Argentina or southern Africa are the coldest ones in the United States.

If you could travel from the Tropic of Cancer to the North Pole, you'd find that summer days are longer the farther north you go. Near the North Pole, in fact, the sun shines for twenty-four hours at the summer solstice. Arctic regions are called the land of the midnight sun.

Visitors to Alaska must have trouble sleeping on summer

nights when the sun never sets. On the other hand, it might be hard to get up in the morning in midwinter when there is almost no sunshine during the day.

Even though it's the beginning of the summer season, the summer solstice is often called Midsummer Day. Maybe this is because it is the longest day of the year, and after the summer solstice the days begin to get shorter. Midsummer Day was an important religious festival in ancient cultures that worshiped the sun. And on Midsummer Night spirits were believed to roam the world.

Janama Ashtmi

In July Hindus celebrate the birth of Lord Krishna. Krishna is one incarnation of the god Vishnu and his adventures and victories are told in the sacred writings of Hinduism. The story of his birth says that his uncle planned to kill him because soothsayers said the child would cause his death. But another child was substituted for Krishna as soon as he was born, so Krishna escaped death. Music and colorful processions through the streets mark the festival of Janama Ashtmi.

Festival of Lanterns

Some Buddhists, especially in Japan, celebrate the Festival of Lanterns in July. This ancient Buddhist ceremony tells people to remember their ancestors. Shrines to ancestors are decorated and people go to cemeteries to take care of their families' graves. The holiday is named for the lanterns that light the streets and guide the ancestral spirits home. Bonfires are lit and dancing and music fill the streets.

Native American Religion

In the United States today there are about 2 million Native Americans who belong to about 230 nations. Native Americans are the people who were in the Americas before the Europeans arrived. They are also called American Indians, because Columbus mistakenly thought he had found a westward route from Europe to the Indies. People soon realized that Columbus had reached a new continent, but the name "Indians" continued to be used.

Native Americans lived in every part of the country. Each group had its own language and developed its own spiritual view of the world. There is no organized religion that is common to all Native Americans.

Native American religions were generally based on belief in spirits who influenced what happened in nature and among human beings. Prayers and rituals were ways of communicating with the spirits. Many of the nations believed in an all-powerful force or great spirit that gave life to all beings. This spirit linked all living things. Nature was a gift from this great spirit, and people had a responsibility to care for all of nature. For Native Americans, religion was not separate from everyday life; it was involved in every activity and thought people had.

Many Native Americans today practice the old religions of their ancestors. Others have found ways to combine their ancient beliefs with those of religions imported from other parts of the world, such as Christianity. In nearly every part of the United States Native Americans gather at some time during the year; some of these celebrations are primarily religious occasions, while others include both religious and secular events.

Seminoles, for example, have a Green Corn Celebration in late June or early July with dancing and feasting for all and religious observances by men and boys. Zunis in the Southwest have a winter festival for the Shalako, who are messengers of the rain spirits; masked dancers perform chants and pray for rain. In the Great Plains and Rocky Mountains, several nations such as Utes, Shoshones, Crees, Sioux, and Cheyennes perform sun dances in the summer when a man is told in a dream to do so.

Celebrations that are known as powwows or intertribal

ceremonies include several different nations; these gatherings began in the twentieth century. In Oklahoma there is a week-long summer fair with horse races, dance contests, and games and rides. Kiowa, Comanche, Delaware, Osage, Pawnee, Apache, and other Plains nations take part in this annual festival. The Inter-Tribal Indian Ceremonial has been celebrated since 1922 in New Mexico. More than forty different nations have participated in the ceremonial dance part of this event over the years; at least a dozen groups perform traditional dances in authentic costumes every year. The Ceremonial also includes a dance contest, an exhibition of artworks and a craft show, and a rodeo, as well as traditional music and storytelling and lots of Native American food. Everyone, whether Native American or not, is welcome to come to these powwows, but outsiders may not take part in the religious ceremonies, and taping, video recording, and photographing are restricted.

In some parts of the United States a day is set aside each year to be celebrated as American Indian Day. In Arizona, for example, it is the last Friday in September, but in other places this holiday is held at different times. It's a day for powwows, music, dancing, and good food—a day when people show their pride in their Native American heritage.

Other Religions

How many different religions are there in the world? It's almost impossible to answer this question. At least six major religions number more than 15 million followers apiece: Christianity, Islam, Hinduism, Buddhism, Sikhism, Judaism. But there are many more religions whose numbers are smaller. Zoroastrianism, for example, which began in ancient Persia, is practiced by well over a quarter of a million people.

It's sometimes hard too to separate out one particular religion's population. In China, for example, many people follow all three of the historic religions of that country

(Buddhism, Confucianism, and Taoism) and they may also celebrate holidays based on even earlier beliefs. In India, Sikhism and Jainism both arose out of Hindu beliefs. Sikhs and Jains don't really think of themselves as Hindus, but they are often included in population totals for Hinduism. Shintoism is the ancient religion of Japan, but many people in that country go to both Shinto and Buddhist temples and observe festivals of both religions.

People from all over the world came to North America, and their cultures and religions make up the rich multicultural heritage we all share. In the United States most of us live and work with people of various religions. You probably have friends and classmates whose religious backgrounds are different from yours. Take advantage of this opportunity! It's fascinating to learn about the wide variety of beliefs that people live by. You're likely to find that many religions share the same ideas in different forms.

Perhaps you already invite friends of other faiths to celebrate holidays with your family. And maybe you'll find ways to adapt some of their traditions to your holiday festivities. After all, the ways people celebrate have already changed over the centuries to fit into different places and different times. Adding new foods or decorations or songs and games to your celebrations enriches your life and makes the holidays more fun.

July 4

Independence Day

Most people know why the fourth of July is called Independence Day. It's because the Declaration of Independence was signed on July 4, 1776. The colonies in North America at that time were ruled by England, but many of the colonists had become unhappy with this arrangement. They were particularly upset that while the taxes they had to pay to England kept increasing, they had no representatives in England's Parliament to express their point of view. "No taxation without representation" was an idea that more and more people supported. But England refused to listen.

As unrest and discontent grew in the colonies, England's King George III sent more troops to control any signs of rebellion. In 1774 the colonies sent delegates to Philadelphia to form the First Continental Congress. The delegates were unhappy with England, but no one wanted to declare war.

In April, 1775, British troops started toward Concord, Massachusetts, to take over a supply of weapons the colonists had stored there. Minutemen (colonists who had volunteered to be ready for military service at a minute's notice) were warned by Paul Revere that the British were coming. "The shot heard round the world" began the battle that marked the unofficial beginning of the war.

In May the Second Continental Congress began. For more than a year the delegates tried to solve their problems with England without declaring war. But by June, 1776, many delegates thought it was hopeless. A committee was formed to compose a formal declaration of independence; one of its members, Thomas Jefferson, wrote the actual document.

On July 2 the delegates of the colonies voted for independence and on July 4 the Declaration of Independence was signed. A new nation, the United States of America, had been born.

The Declaration of Independence opens with one of the most famous sentences in the world. Now, more than two centuries later, these words are as important and meaningful as they were to the colonists in 1776. "We hold these truths to be self-evident, that all Men are created equal, that they are endowed by their Creator with certain unalienable Rights, that among these are Life, Liberty, and the Pursuit of Happiness."

Even on the first Fourth of July celebration, held in 1777, there was lots of noise. Bells rang all day and ships fired their cannons to salute the thirteen colonies. By the early 1800s the traditions of parades, picnics, and fireworks were firmly established. Then as now, marching bands played patriotic music. A favorite has always been "Yankee Doodle," which was played by the soldiers' fifes and drums during the Revolutionary War.

The Fourth of July is a noisy, joyous celebration. Although private fireworks have been banned in many places because they are so dangerous, towns and cities usually have big fireworks displays that all the citizens can watch. Most towns have Fourth of July parades with bands, marching community groups, and lots of flags. Families have picnics and barbecues, often with larger groups. And everyone has a lot of fun celebrating our country's birthday.

Did You Know . . . ?

An amazing coincidence occurred on July 4, 1826. While the nation observed the fiftieth Independence Day, two signers of the Declaration of Independence died peacefully at their homes in Massachusetts and Virginia. John Adams, our second president, was ninety and Thomas Jefferson, our third president, was eighty-three. Both men were very important figures in the move toward independence from England and the forming of our country. In an age when many people died young, it must have been wonderful for them to live long enough to see fifty years of their new nation.

*

Did you ever wonder where Uncle Sam came from? A man named Sam Wilson who lived in Troy, New York, dealt with army supplies during the War of 1812. He was called Uncle Sam by many people in his community, and one of his workers said jokingly that the initials U.S. (for United States) that were stamped on each barrel of army supplies really stood for "Uncle Sam." Soon the expression became popular, as soldiers talked about fighting Uncle Sam's war and eating Uncle Sam's meat in the army. Sam Wilson probably didn't look anything like the tall, thin, bearded figure in striped clothes that was drawn later in the nineteenth century by the cartoonist Thomas Nast. But his name is still famous today.

*

How would you like to have a turkey as your national symbol? That's what Benjamin Franklin wanted. When others suggested an eagle, because eagles have traditionally been symbols of power, Franklin objected. He said they had "bad moral character" because they stole food from weaker birds. On the other hand, he said, "The turkey is in comparison a much more respectable bird, a true original native of America."

Congress did eventually choose the eagle, but it chose the bald eagle, which is found only in North America.

CELEBRATE!

Flags on Parade

Wouldn't it be fun to put on your own Fourth of July parade? It's a great way to celebrate this cheerful holiday with your friends. Gather up as many participants as you can find. In a parade, the more the merrier.

You'll want to hold your parade where other people can watch and enjoy themselves too. March around the backyard while everyone is waiting for Dad to finish barbecueing. Or if several families are picnicking in the park, you could have it there. And, of course, if your town holds a Fourth of July parade every year, your group can probably join in. Ask the mayor in advance so you'll know where to meet.

What about costumes? Most people in a parade wear a costume or uniform and for the Fourth of July there are lots of possibilities for costumes with patriotic themes. If you've got striped pants and a tailcoat, you can make a top hat out of cardboard and go as Uncle Sam. But why not do something that all of you can be part of?

You need thirteen people to represent the original thirteen colonies. Each person wears a blue T-shirt with a big white star on the front of it. Make the star out of plain white paper and pin it to the shirt. Then each of you can make a stand-up headband for your colony. Cut a strip of lightweight cardboard about two inches wide and long enough to fit around your head. Cut out letters (several inches tall) to spell your colony's name. Color the letters and headband red or blue and tape or staple the letters to the headband.

The stars on your shirts represent the stars of the first American flag, and all of you will carry the stripes. To make these you'll need seven strips of red and six strips of white crepe paper, each about twenty-four feet long. Also cut out

View from rear of human flag

staples

cardboard

cardboard

cardboard

↑
crepe paper

and so on until you
have 13 cardboard strips

and so on until
you have 13 people

ASSEMBLING A HUMAN FLAG

thirteen strips of posterboard or other light cardboard; make each of them one inch wide and thirty inches long.

Staple one end of each crepe paper streamer in alternating colors down one of the cardboard strips. Be sure to begin and end with red so your human flag will look like the real one. Then unroll about two feet of each streamer and staple them to another cardboard strip. Don't worry that you have to push the streamers' edges to the side to get your stapler in position; the crepe paper will spring back into shape. Keep stapling the crepe paper flag's stripes to the cardboard strips until you get to the end. Now each of you will have a cardboard strip to hold as you carry your flag.

If your parade route has room, all thirteen of you can walk side by side holding the flag stripes in front of you. If not, walk single file carrying the stripes at your side. Either way, you'll be the most creative part of the parade.

Patriot's Cake

A great addition to any Fourth of July picnic is a flag cake, and it's super easy to make. Use any white or yellow cake mix (not angel food) and bake it in a rectangular pan about nine by thirteen inches. When it's cool, you're ready to frost it like a flag.

PATRIOT'S CAKE

Spread either white frosting or whipped cream cheese all over the top of the cake. In the upper left corner use blue-berries to make a blue square about five inches on each side. Then put a circle of thirteen mini-marshmallows on the blue-berries to represent the stars on the first U.S. flag.

Red stripes are the only ones you have to make, because the white frosting will become the white ones. Use slices of strawberries unless you have a bunch of raspberries handy. With a table knife, draw lines for the stripes on the frosting. Starting at the top, lay a stripe of red, leave space for the white stripe, and then make another one of red. The first seven stripes go next to the blue square and the other six go all the way across underneath it.

You'll be the hit of the picnic and everyone will want a piece of this delicious "flag." If you've got a big group coming, maybe you'd better make two!

August 13

International Lefthanders Day

International Lefthanders Day was created in 1976. The date of August 13 was chosen as a way of making fun of superstitions (that year it was a Friday the 13th).

Being lefthanded has long been considered strange. In Ireland some people believed that lefthanders were friends of the leprechauns and fairies who abound in Irish legends. Other people think that a lefthanded person brings bad luck. Lots of words reflect this idea. *Sinister*, which means "evil" or "ominous," started out as a Latin word meaning "left." *Gauche*, which we think of as meaning "lacking in social skills," is really the French word for "left." In fact, the word *left* itself comes from an Old English word that meant "weak" or "worthless."

Some common phrases carry out this same theme. If you have two left feet, you're clumsy, and if you receive a lefthanded compliment, you'll want to look for the double meaning that makes it almost an insult.

While being lefthanded won't really bring you bad luck, it is kind of unlucky in lots of ways. All kinds of things in daily life are made for righthanded people. Scissors and can open-

179

ers are made to work for righties, watch stems are placed on the right of the watch face so a rightie can easily reset the time, piano keys are arranged so that the right hand plays the melody, and most lefties have to get special lefthanded golf clubs in order to play the game.

In addition, lefthanded people often have trouble finding someone to teach them new skills. It's hard for a rightie to teach a leftie how to knit or crochet or how to hold a baseball bat. And if you think about shaking hands, you can see how the world is geared for righthanded people.

The people who started International Lefthanders Day wanted a special day to help create a positive attitude toward lefthandedness. They encourage people to celebrate this day with lefthanded baseball games and golf tournaments and with gatherings and parades of lefties. Lefthanders International publishes *Lefthander Magazine* as well as a catalog of items redesigned for lefthanders.

Did You Know . . . ?

Redesigning things for lefties is not a new idea. In the fifteenth century there was a Scots-Irish family named Kerr. (*Kerr* comes from the Gaelic word for "left.") There were so many lefties in that family that in 1470 they built a special spiral staircase in their castle. Normally on a spiral staircase, you walk counterclockwise on the way up and clockwise on the way down. This worked well for righthanded swordsmen defending the upper floors, because they had room to swing their swords. But it wasn't so great for most of the Kerr family, so their staircase spiraled in the reverse direction.

*

Although lefthanders make up only 10 to 15 percent of the population, there are a lot of famous ones. Lefthanded leaders in history include Alexander the Great, Julius Caesar, Joan of Arc, and Napoleon. Lefties are often thought to be more creative than righthanded people. There were famous artists, such as Michelangelo and Leonardo da Vinci; well-known authors, such as Lewis Carroll and Mark Twain; and inventor Thomas Edison. So if you are lefthanded, you're in good company.

*

Lefthanders have a definite advantage in baseball. Almost half the batters in baseball's Hall of Fame are lefties or switch hitters. Leftie batters, who stand to the right of home plate, have a shorter distance to run to first base when they hit the ball. And southpaw pitchers don't turn their backs on first base during their windup the way righties do. This means it's easier for them to keep a runner at first from stealing second.

Why are lefthanded people often called southpaws? It originated on the baseball field. Early baseball diamonds always had home plate in the west corner so the afternoon sun wouldn't be in the batter's eyes. As he faced the batter, the pitcher's left arm was toward the south. Thus a pitcher who used his left arm to pitch was called a southpaw.

CELEBRATE!

Southpaw for a Day

The perfect way to celebrate International Lefthanders Day is to spend the entire day doing everything with the hand you don't usually use. That means if you're a rightie, you'll brush your teeth, button and zip your clothes, and pour your milk and eat your cereal with your left hand. (Of course, if you're already a leftie, you'll be doing all these things with your right hand.)

What else is hard to do with the "wrong" hand? Try turning the combination lock on your bike chain or combing your hair. And, of course, even sports you're good at will be a lot harder today.

Try an experiment. First thing in the morning, write out your name, address, and phone number on a piece of paper, using the wrong hand. Did you find the letters easier to make than the numbers, or vice versa? Be sure to keep this piece of paper. After you've spent the morning doing things as a southpaw or northpaw, write out the same information again at lunchtime and see if you've improved. How long do you think it would take you to write well with the other hand? Try it again at night and check the results. This experiment will give you a lot of sympathy for a kid who's broken his hand and has to learn to use the other one while it's mending.

Some people are both right- and lefthanded. Are you one of them? Very few people are truly ambidextrous, which means they can do everything equally well with either hand. More common is the person who writes with his left hand but throws a ball with his right or the other way around. If you normally use your left for some things and your right for others, be sure to use the opposite hand for those activities on International Lefthanders Day.

It's fun to celebrate International Lefthanders Day with a bunch of your friends. You can all keep track of how many times you had to give up and use your regular hand to unlock the door or open a soda can. And at least you'll all be equally clumsy in whatever sport you play on this holiday.

You're Doing It Backward!

Lefthandedness doesn't really mean doing things backward, but sometimes that's how it feels to lefties, especially when they're trying to learn to knit or play the guitar from a book written for righties. This is the perfect day to practice speaking backward. If you get good at it, you and your friends can have whole conversations and no one else will know what you're talking about.

Start with your name—how does it sound if you say it backward? "Carol," for example, becomes "Lorac," which isn't too hard to pronounce. With other names, like "Elizabeth," you'll have to be inventive to say them out loud—"Htebazile"? Sometimes your name said backward takes on a whole different feeling. "Lorac" sounds kind of like a science fiction character, while "Htebazile" might be an ancient Babylonian. Maybe you'll write a story someday with your backward-name character in it.

How about your family—what do their names sound like backward? See if they know who you're talking to when you call them. Your brother Greg might not notice the difference when you call him Gerg, but Jim might not recognize himself as Mij.

"Mom" and "Dad," of course, are reversible names. Words and phrases that read the same in both directions are called palindromes. Several names, such as Eve, Anna, Hannah, and Ada, are palindromes that will be easy to remember in your backward language.

Practice talking backward with your friends; you might make a list of important words you'll want to memorize. Then when you tell your friend, "Stel og teg eci maerc," your mom won't say, "No, it's too close to dinnertime"; she won't know where you're going!

Lefthanded and Proud of It

Tell the world you're a lefty! You can make your own "lefty badge" that says "Don't be left out!" or "Be kind to lefties" or "Lefthanded and proud of it." Use a self-stick removable note sheet or a peel-off label to make your badge, and think up as many clever lefty slogans as you can.

You can use the same self-stick notes to let your whole neighborhood know it's International Lefthanders Day. Since these notes don't damage property, you can stick them on doors, windows, mirrors, or even on lunchboxes and briefcases. Imagine Dad's surprise when he starts to shave in the morning and finds a note on the bathroom mirror that says, "Lefty was here!"

August 19

National Aviation Day

National Aviation Day is celebrated not, as you might guess, on December 17, the date of the Wright brothers' first successful airplane flight in 1903, but on the birthday of Orville Wright. (Maybe people thought we needed another holiday in August, while we already had enough holidays in December.)

Wilbur and Orville Wright were not the first to look for a way for people to fly through the air. Flying had been a dream for many inventors through the centuries, and at least two other men had made and flown engine-powered flying machines before the Wrights. However, none of these earlier planes could stay up in the air after taking off.

Wilbur Wright was born on April 16, 1867; his brother Orville was born on August 19, 1871. As children they were fascinated with machines, and they made and sold homemade mechanical toys to earn money. In their twenties they began renting and selling bicycles, and soon they were manufacturing their own bicycles. In about 1896 they read about Otto Lilienthal, a German inventor who had been experimenting with flying in gliders. The idea of flying sparked their imagination, and they started reading everything they

184

could find about aeronautics and playing around with kites and gliders.

The Wright brothers soon decided that the information about aeronautics that was available to them was totally inaccurate. For many months they experimented in a wind tunnel they built themselves; they also made numerous trial runs with gliders at a sandy hill near Kitty Hawk, North Carolina. Finally they were ready to construct their power airplane. The *Flyer* weighed about 750 pounds, including the pilot, and on December 17, 1903, it flew 852 feet in 59 seconds. Though not many people realized it, the age of the airplane had begun.

Wilbur and Orville Wright continued to improve on their early planes for several years. By 1905 they had solved some steering problems of their airplanes, and in that year Wilbur flew for 38 minutes without any stops.

After Wilbur died of typhoid fever in 1912, Orville worked on his own (he died in 1948). They received many awards and honors, and a National Monument named for them is in North Carolina, where they made their first flights. Their original plane is in the National Air and Space Museum in Washington, D.C. It looks flimsy and old-fashioned to our eyes today, but every airplane in the world is based on the same principles of flight that made the Wright brothers' *Flyer* fly.

Did You Know . . . ?

Before the invention of engines to drive machines, true flight was impossible for humans. But people had come up with ingenious ways to "fly," or to float above the ground. One of the most popular ways to fly was ballooning.

The first balloons that could lift a basket carrying a person were hot-air balloons. Joseph and Etienne Montgolfier, brothers who lived in France, came up with the idea of using a flame to inflate a huge balloon with hot air. Because hot air rises, it filled the balloon and then lifted it into the air. Their first balloon carrying two men was launched in 1783 and it landed successfully after about twenty-five minutes.

Only ten days later, on December 1, 1783, another French inventor named Jacques Alexandre Cesar Charles made a successful flight using a balloon filled with hydrogen.

Ballooning can be dangerous, but many people today go ballooning for sport, using hot-air balloons. Watching the huge nylon balloon slowly puff up with air and begin to pull at the ropes that hold it to the earth makes us powerfully aware of the natural forces around us.

*

Would it surprise you to learn that neither Wilbur nor Orville Wright went to college? They both went through high school, but they didn't get their diplomas. The Wrights are examples of self-taught inventors who got interested in an idea and learned all about it by reading everything that was available. Their experiments and inventions were based on a great deal of research; for example, they tested more than two hundred different types of wings in their wind tunnel in their search for the best design for their airplane.

The "knowledge explosion" of the twentieth century has made it much more difficult to be a self-taught scientist. So much more has been learned and discovered in every field of science and mathematics that it would be nearly impossible to learn all of it on your own.

CELEBRATE!

Design a Plane

Like Wilbur and Orville Wright, you can do a series of experiments to find out what is the most successful shape and weight for an airplane. The only thing you need to know to get started is how to make a traditional paper airplane.

Fold a sheet of regular typewriter paper in half the long way. Then open it up flat with the fold facing down. Fold the

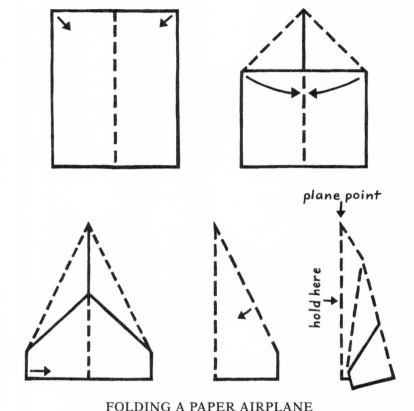

FOLDING A PAPER AIRPLANE

two top corners in until they touch each other at the center fold line. Now fold these same sections in again so that the new corners meet at the center fold line.

Fold the plane in half on the center fold line you made first. Then fold the side pieces down to form the wings.

Now get ready for your experiments. First fly the plane just the way it is. How far does it go? Does it go straight for a while and then down, or does it head down right away? What happens when you throw it in different ways—straight up into the air, at an upward angle, gently or with lots of power? Keep notes on your results so you can compare them with later experiments.

Next, try making some changes in your plane's design. You might add weight to various parts of it—attach paper clips to the nose, the wings, or the underside, and see how this affects the plane's ability to fly. Now try folding the wings in a different shape. You can adjust the fold lines to make the wings slope down toward the rear of the plane; you can fold the wings twice to make them narrower. Fool around and see what other ideas you come up with. For instance, you might make several very narrow folds at the nose end of the paper before you start making the airplane; how does this affect the airplane's flight?

How else can you test the design of paper airplanes? Maybe you'd like to start by comparing large, medium, and small planes. Or you could make planes the same size but different weights, using thin paper, construction paper, and light-weight cardboard. You could make planes out of foil or out of two different materials; for example, you could tape card-board wings to a paper body or vice versa. And why not try making a plane out of a paper plate? The shape will be quite different even though it's constructed in the same way.

The more you play around with paper airplanes, the more unusual ideas you'll come up with for experimenting. And who knows? Maybe you'll discover something brand-new about the science of flight!

Make Your Own Airmail

Now that you've got some terrific paper airplanes, why not fly some of them to your friends? Just unfold a plane (care-fully, so it doesn't rip) and write a letter on the unfolded paper. When you're finished, fold the plane along enough of its fold lines so it will lie flat and fit into an envelope (you may need a fairly large one). Seal it up and send it off—your friend will be impressed with your talent at airplane design-ing!

This "airplane stationery" combines a toy with a short note. Send one to Grandpa for his birthday or to Cousin Sue when she graduates from nursing school. You don't have to write a long letter; just "Happy Birthday" or "Congratulations" might be enough. Paper planes are fun for people of all ages to fly.

Feeding Your Feathered Friends

Long before humans could fly, birds of all sorts swooped gracefully through the air using their own muscle power. It's interesting to watch different kinds of birds; some seem to float and hover in the air, while others dart and dive, moving their wings rapidly as they go. Why not give the birds in your backyard a snacking spot where you can observe their varying methods of flying as they come and go? This easy-to-make bird feeder is also easy to keep full of seeds, stale bread and cake crumbs, and an occasional handful of raisins.

All you need is an empty coffee can and two plastic lids to fit it, a wire coat hanger, a stick or rod that's longer than

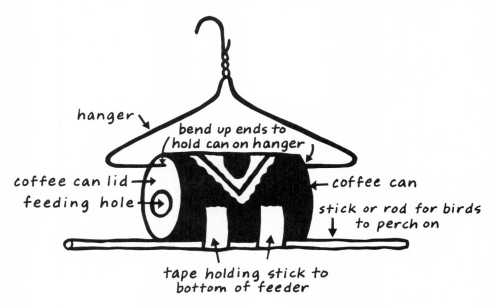

MAKING A BIRD FEEDER

the coffee can, and some strong tape. Cut a round hole in the center of each plastic lid, an inch or so in diameter. Use a can opener to cut off the bottom of the coffee can; put one of the lids on each end.

Using a wire clipper, remove about four inches from the middle of the horizontal part of the coat hanger. Poke the cut ends into the plastic lids near the edge; it's easiest to do this step with the lids on the can. Now take the hanger out again and use pliers to bend about 1/2 inch of each cut end up; when you stick the hanger back through these small holes, the bends will keep the can from sliding off the hanger.

Tape the stick to the bottom of the feeder—the ends that stick out past the edges of the can will give the birds a place to perch while they eat.

Fill the feeder, but make sure there's not so much food that it spills out through the large feeding holes. Hang it on a tree limb or high hook and wait for your feathered friends to discover it!

August 26

Women's Equality Day

Women's Equality Day celebrates the date when the Nineteenth Amendment to the Constitution of the United States was passed in 1920. This amendment gave women the right to vote.

It's hard to imagine that less than one hundred years ago women were not allowed to vote. It's even harder to believe that it took more than seventy years of hard work, from 1848 to 1920, to confer this basic right on half the population. But that's what happened.

Although a number of famous women had written and spoken on this vital issue for years, the women's suffrage movement (suffrage means the right to vote) first got organized in July 1848, in Seneca Falls, New York. Elizabeth Cady Stanton led the first U.S. women's rights convention in adopting a Declaration of Principles, modeled on the Declaration of Independence. It began, "We hold these truths to be self-evident, that all men and women are created equal. . . ." The first demand that this Declaration made was for women's right to vote, because without that, women would have no power to correct other injustices.

191

In those days women had practically no rights. Most states wouldn't allow divorced women to have custody of their children. Married women in many states had no control over their own property or earnings. Women weren't allowed to be jurors or even witnesses in a court. A man was responsible for his wife's actions and had the right to punish her as he saw fit.

These things seem unbelievable to us now. So why did it take so long for women to get the right to vote and be full-fledged citizens? In part it was because things had been this way for so long that men (who were the ones voting) couldn't see a need for change. In addition, in the nineteenth century people who believed in women's suffrage tended to be people who were against slavery. Many thought they could change only one of these injustices at a time and the women would have to wait until blacks got their rights. Others, like Elizabeth Cady Stanton and her comrade-in-arms Susan B. Anthony, thought there was no need to wait on either question. This split among the people working for equality lessened their power.

The women's rights movement also became connected with the temperance, or antidrinking, movement, which was first organized by women. The liquor industry feared that if women got the vote, they would pass laws against drinking. This powerful group worked hard to prevent women from becoming equal citizens.

Nevertheless, the Nineteenth Amendment was passed by both the House of Representatives and the Senate. That wasn't the end, though; the amendment had to be ratified by thirty-six of the states in order to become part of the Constitution. One by one, thirty-five states accepted the new amendment. At last, on August 26, 1920, the last ratification needed (Tennessee's) was received in Washington, D.C. Finally women would be able to vote along with men.

Did You Know . . . ?

Tennessee's ratification of the Nineteenth Amendment was a hard-fought campaign and it looked as though it would be a tie vote in Tennessee's House of Representatives. But twenty-four-year-old Representative Harry Burns decided to vote in favor of ratification even though his district opposed it. He had promised his mother he would do this if his vote was needed to break the tie. He said, "I appreciated the fact that an opportunity such as seldom comes to a mortal man to free seventeen million women from political slavery was mine."

*

The liquor industry was worried that women might get the right to vote. It secretly raised money to help politicians who were against women's suffrage. In Texas in 1913 the Brewers' Association and the liquor distillers worked to raise more than 8 million dollars to defeat the proposal for women's suffrage in that state. In Ohio too, the liquor industry collected 8 million dollars in 1914 and managed to defeat women's suffrage there. That was a lot of money to raise just to keep women from voting. Spending 8 million dollars in 1914 was about the same as spending 114 million dollars in 1990.

*

In the 1860s women couldn't vote anywhere in the United States. But in Wyoming, which was still a Territory, Mrs. Esther Morris persuaded the Territorial Council to introduce a bill giving women there the right to vote. The bill was passed and the governor signed it in 1869. Mrs. Morris went on to become a judge. No one back east seemed to care what happened out west. However, when Wyoming asked to become a state twenty years later, politicians got worried. For a while it looked as though Wyoming would have to choose between keeping women's suffrage and becoming a state. But Wyoming's legislature said, "We will remain out of the

Union one hundred years rather than come in without the women." Wyoming was admitted to the Union in 1890.

CELEBRATE!

A Debate for Equality

The question of whether women should have the right to vote was debated by many politicians as they ran for office in the nineteenth century. Debates were an important part of political campaigns and they are still held today before many elections. And though women's suffrage is no longer a question, there are still lots of issues concerning women's equality that are debated and discussed.

Why don't you organize a debate in your class, at camp, or at your community center? It's an interesting way to learn about important issues and it's good practice for presenting your ideas in a way that will convince others. In formal debates, there are specific rules to be followed, but you can present an informal debate that will be easier. The main idea is that there is a "proposition" to be debated, and two teams of debaters. One team is the affirmative team, which is in favor of the proposition; the other is the negative team, which is against it.

Each team researches the issue and prepares its ideas and arguments. You can decide how many speakers you want on each side and how long they will speak. One way is to have the person chosen by the affirmative team speak first for five minutes. Then the person chosen by the negative team speaks for five minutes. Each of these speakers presents the arguments for his or her team.

Next come the rebuttals—speeches in which each team tries to counter the arguments made by the other team. The second speaker for the affirmative team might have five minutes for the rebuttal, and then the negative team's second speaker would have five minutes also.

People who enjoy debating often present ideas that they

don't believe in themselves. They like the process of organizing their ideas in a persuasive argument, whether or not they go along with these ideas. One good thing about arguing a case you don't believe in is that it makes you more aware of the reasons behind other people's positions on important issues.

In your debate about women's issues, it's important not to have only girls on one team and boys on the other. A mix of boys and girls on both sides makes your position stronger, whichever side you take.

What issues should you debate? Of course, you can do some research about women's suffrage and present a debate that might have taken place before 1920. But there are plenty of other women's rights questions that people still disagree about. Should women fight in armed combat on the front lines? Should women be able to work at all the same jobs as men? Is a woman capable of being president of the United States?

Maybe you'd prefer to debate an issue that's closer to you. Perhaps most of the sports teams in your school are boys' teams. Should the school provide as much practice space and money for girls' teams as for boys'? Should girls be allowed to play on the boys' teams? Maybe most people in your class do certain kinds of chores at home. Should girls always do the dishes and boys always take out the trash? Talk it over in class and see if there are other questions that would make good debating issues.

When debates are held, there is a judge (or more than one) who listens to the arguments and decides which team has argued its side best. For a class debate, the students who are not taking part in the debate will be the judges. After it's over, they can vote on which team presented its case the best. Remember, the judges don't have to agree with the arguments; they just have to decide which point of view was most convincingly presented.

Debates are a great way to exercise your brain and to examine your own beliefs and ideas. And who knows, maybe you'll argue so well that your audience will look at an issue from a point of view they've never considered before.

Celebrate the Debate

After your debate, or just as a celebration of Women's Equality Day, it's fun for you and your friends to have a 1920s-style tea. You can serve old-fashioned foods that were popular when real women's suffrage debates were held. An easy-to-prepare menu could include melon boats, ribbon sandwiches, old-fashioned root-beer floats, and "equality cupcakes."

Melon boats

For the melon boats you'll need a ripe cantaloupe or honeydew melon and some other small fruit, such as strawberries, cut-up watermelon, and grapes. Cut the cantaloupe in half (be careful when using a sharp knife and ask an adult to help if necessary). First take out the seeds. Then, with a melon baller or teaspoon, scoop out the fruit from both melon halves and put these small chunks into a big bowl. Add squares of watermelon, washed strawberries and grapes, and whatever other fruit you're using. Gently mix the fruit pieces and then spoon it all back into the melon halves. Since you'll have more fruit than you took out of the original melons, you can heap the melon "boats" high and still have leftover fruit to put in a bowl.

Ribbon sandwiches

Ribbon sandwiches are pretty and easy to make. For each set of tiny sandwiches, you'll need three slices of bread. Spread two of the bread slices with any filling you like. A traditional favorite is cream cheese on one and strawberry jam on another; or you could try deviled ham for one layer and egg salad for the other. The ribbon effect comes from using different colors in the same set of sandwiches, so you

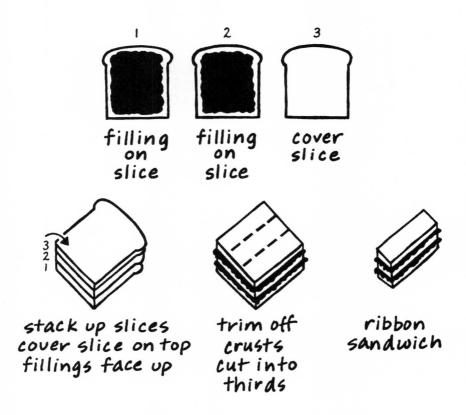

MAKING RIBBON SANDWICHES

might want to use white and brown bread as well as different colors of filling.

After you've put together your double-decker sandwiches, carefully slice off the bread crusts on all four sides of each one (ask before using a sharp knife). Then cut each large sandwich into three skinny ones. When you turn the various ribbon tea sandwiches on their sides, you'll have a pretty rainbow effect.

Root-beer floats

Root-beer floats are super simple. All you need are tall glasses, ice cream, root beer, and straws. Root beer poured over vanilla ice cream in a tall glass is a traditional root-beer float; if you use chocolate ice cream, it still tastes great but it's called a "black cow."

"Equality cupcakes"

Plain cupcakes are transformed into "equality cupcakes" by making equals signs with frosting on the top of each one. Use your favorite cake mix or make cupcakes from scratch (be sure you have permission to use the oven). Frost them when they're cool with whatever frosting you like best. Then use a contrasting color frosting to make an equals sign on each cupcake.

*

Now invite all your friends to tea, and play some ragtime music from the 1920s in the background. Happy Women's Equality Day!

Labor Day

In the nineteenth century, life in the United States was transformed by the Industrial Revolution, which had begun a century earlier in England. The Industrial Revolution wasn't a war or even a specific event. It was a series of changes that came about between 1750 and 1850 when new inventions led to people working in factories. Before this time, most things were manufactured by hand. But when James Watt invented the steam engine, machines could be built to manufacture all sorts of things. These same changes spread to other countries, including the United States.

Factories meant a new kind of worker—someone who worked at the same job every day at a factory, not on a farm or in a small shop where things were made by hand. It's hard to imagine today what kinds of working conditions these early factory workers endured. Factory work was hard and dangerous and people worked long hours for little pay. If they protested, they lost their jobs.

Eventually workers united to form labor unions. Their goal was to improve working conditions in the factories. During this struggle there was a lot of anger and hostility between the workers and the owners of the factories. Few owners

199

were happy about making changes, such as increased pay and shorter hours, that would cost their companies money. Workers, of course, felt that they deserved fair pay and safe working conditions in return for their labor.

In 1882 a union leader in New York City named Peter J. McGuire had the idea of starting a holiday that would honor working people. Other unions thought this was a good plan and on September 5, 1882, the first Labor Day celebration was held. More than ten thousand workers marched in a giant parade through the streets of New York and afterward there were picnics and fireworks.

McGuire's idea caught on, and by 1893 thirty states had made the first Monday in September a holiday. The following year it became a national holiday.

There are still parades on Labor Day in most places and always lots of picnics. Labor Day signals the end of summer and for many kids it's the beginning of the school year.

Did You Know . . . ?

In 1897 Peter J. McGuire wrote about the beginnings of Labor Day and how he chose the date for it. He said, "[I] suggested the first Monday in September of every year for such a holiday, as it would come at the most pleasant season of the year—nearly midway between the Fourth of July and Thanksgiving, and would fill a wide gap in the chronology of legal holidays." Wouldn't it be nice if all our holidays had been evenly arranged through the year?

*

What did the first Labor Day marchers care most about? The banners they carried in the parade give some hints. "Vote for the Labor Ticket" and "The True Remedy Is Organization and the Ballot" tell us that unions encouraged their members to vote for politicians who supported their ideas. The slogan "8 Hours Constitute a Day's Work" suggests that working conditions were still a vital issue. Look for books with photos of long-ago Labor Day parades to see what other ideas were important. Then look at newspaper photos or television coverage of today's Labor Day parades to see if marchers still have the same concerns.

CELEBRATE!

The Key to Success Is Hard Work!

Peter McGuire, who founded Labor Day, was head of the United Brotherhood of Carpenters and Joiners of America. To celebrate Labor Day, why not do some very simple carpentry and create a key rack the whole family can use?

You can make a simple and inexpensive key rack out of a piece of wood and some cup hooks. In order to decide what size the key rack should be, you have to figure out where it's going to hang when it's finished. Maybe all the members of your family leave their keys near the front door. You could make a rectangular key rack to hang on the inside of the front-hall closet door. Or maybe there are a lot of loose keys jumbled in a kitchen drawer (keys to the garage, basement, toolshed, Grandma's house, bike lock, or extra keys to the family cars). Wouldn't it be great to have them all lined up and labeled? Your key rack might be long and narrow to fit on the kitchen wall under the cabinets. Talk it over with your mom and dad and decide on a good spot to hang everyone's keys.

The wood you use should be the kind that is sold as 1 inch thick (a 1″ × 4″ board is not actually 1 inch thick—it's closer to ¾″). See if there is a leftover piece of wood lying around your house, or go to a lumberyard and ask if they have some scrap wood you could look through. If it's not the right size, you can probably have it cut to the length you want for a small charge.

When you have the wood, you can paint or stain it a color that will go with the room, or leave it plain if you prefer. (If the wood feels rough, use sandpaper to smooth it so it will look nice.) When it's dry, gather up all the keys that are going to hang on it and arrange them the way you want them. Make pencil marks where the cup hooks should go.

Now it's time to screw in the cup hooks. Sometimes it's hard to start a screw in solid wood; if so, hammer a nail a little way in and then pull it out to provide a starting hole.

Once the cup hooks are in, label the spaces above them. Your labels might say "Mom," "Dad," "Joe," and "Mary," or they might say "Garage," "Side door," "Grandma," and "Bob's bike lock." Use stick-on labels to identify each key's place on the rack. Then you can change them if it's ever necessary. Write the labels neatly in dark pen so they're easy to read.

Hang your new key rack wherever you've decided on. The whole family will thank you every time they're searching for a key.

KEY RACK

Organize Some Labor Day Fun

On Labor Day there's often a picnic or barbecue with lots of kids and adults who come to eat and have a good time as the summer ends. When the eating part is over or while you're waiting for it to start, the kids often don't know exactly what they want to do. Now's your chance to be the games director and organize everyone in some easy outdoor games.

Depending on how many kids are there and how old they are, you can get everyone playing tag, Simon says, or Red Rover. If you plan ahead and bring along some string or rope, you can have a three-legged race. Or what about a wheelbarrow race? That's great for a laugh, especially when the older kids are the wheelbarrows and the little ones are the pushers. A relay race is also easy to organize, and you can use sticks or large pebbles for the batons.

Have you ever heard of ring-o-levio? It's an old game—maybe it was played at the first Labor Day picnic in 1882. But it's still great fun for a group. It's usually played at dusk, so it's a perfect way to wind up the picnic. You need a flashlight and an open area where players can find hiding places.

Pick a tree or other spot to be the base. One person is It, and he or she has the flashlight. To begin the game, It closes his eyes and counts to ten or twenty or whatever number you decide on, saying "One ring-o-levio, two ring-o-levio," and so on. The other players scatter and hide.

When It finishes counting, he turns on the flashlight and goes looking for the other players. When he spots someone, he "tags" her with the flashlight beam and calls out her name. She is then caught and must go to the base, where she is a prisoner. (If It calls the wrong name, the player remains free.) The players can move around as much as they want to while It is searching.

The first prisoner who is caught becomes the Guard of the base and helps It for the rest of the game. Other players that It catches stay at the base as prisoners.

The idea of the game is for It to make everyone a prisoner. But a player can free the prisoners by reaching the base and touching it before being tagged. However, if the Guard tags the player before he reaches the base, he becomes a prisoner too.

If It manages to capture all the players, the game is over and a new It is picked for the next game.

Of course, if you play ring-o-levio in daylight, it's too easy for It to call out the names of players he locates. For a daytime version, you can play that It must touch-tag a player to make him a prisoner. However, to make it fair, you need to make boundaries that the hiding players must stay within.

Whatever games you play on Labor Day, try to make sure that the big kids and the little kids all have some chances to win. That way everyone will enjoy this day of fun and play.

September, first Saturday after Labor Day

Public Lands Day

What are public lands? They are any areas that belong to the government (federal, state, or local) and that therefore belong to all the people. But public lands are not just parks and forests. They include highways, parking lots, playgrounds and school yards, public buildings, and even some sidewalks.

Because places like these don't belong to a specific person or group, often there is nobody who feels responsible for keeping them clean and pretty. But in fact it's everybody's job to make sure they are places we can all be proud of.

A nonprofit organization called Keep America Beautiful, Inc., was founded in 1953 to "keep America beautiful." Its main focus at first was on preventing litter in public places. And while the organization now works on toxic waste problems and other large issues, it still helps other groups and individuals find ways to clean up public lands in their own communities.

Public Lands Day was started as a holiday to make everyone aware of the need to clean up our environment. It's a day to take a look at the public lands around us—rivers, lakes, woods, wildlife refuges, parks, beaches, roads, and public buildings. If these places belonged to you, would you be happy with the way they look? Or would you be upset at the amount of trash that's tossed on the ground, the garbage people throw in the water, the worn and ragged spots in the grass, and the broken tree limbs and scraggly flowers?

Just as most people want their homes to look clean and attractive, most of us want our community lands to be inviting spots to visit. After all, we are the ones who pass by these places every day—how our community looks affects us more than anybody else.

Public Lands Day is the time to get started on doing something about the way our public lands look. You'll be joining with thousands of other concerned people who use this day as a focal point to begin cleanup campaigns that can last all year long.

Did You Know . . . ?

There is an Andrew H. Davison Award for outstanding community activities that support Public Lands Day. It is sponsored by Keep America Beautiful, Inc., along with Take Pride in America. You can write for an application to Keep America Beautiful, Inc., Mill River Plaza, 9 West Broad Street, Stamford, CT 06902.

*

We produce over 175 million tons of household and commercial waste each year—that's almost four pounds of trash for every man, woman and child in this country every day. About 40 percent of our trash is paper and almost 20 percent is stuff from yards and parks, like leaves and grass clippings. One third of the nation's landfill capacity will be totally used up by the year 2000; in many places *all* the space in landfills is already filled up with trash.

*

People have become more aware of the litter problem in recent years, and many cities have antilitter laws and fines for those who do litter. Still, litter is a serious problem. One thing that seems to make littering worse is the "copycat" syndrome. When people see a bunch of trash blown against a fence or building or heaped up in the gutter, they don't feel bad about adding to it. After all, they think, the place is already a mess, so who cares if I make it worse?

This means that when you clean up a public place, you're helping in two ways. Not only are you making it look better right away; you're helping it stay that way, because people won't be as quick to throw the first piece of trash in a place that looks nice.

CELEBRATE!

Adopt a Public Land

The idea of "adopting" a public place and keeping it free of litter is not brand-new. Maybe you've seen signs along highways that say Adopt A Highway. Many community organizations choose stretches of highway or sections of parks; their members take turns on weekends cleaning up these areas. But there are plenty of unadopted places that need sponsors.

Your class or club or scout troop can choose a piece of public land to take care of. It might be the playground at your school, or a part of your local park, or even a block of city sidewalk. And the perfect time to start your adoption is Public Lands Day.

First you'll need to find out if this kind of program is already in effect. If it is, which areas have already been adopted? If it isn't, maybe you and your friends can get the idea going, not only for your group but for other groups in your town. The mayor's office or the Chamber of Commerce will probably know about whatever is going on; call or visit and tell them what you plan to do. At school, explain the idea to your principal and ask for help in publicizing your project.

If you're adopting a city sidewalk, talk to the people who live on that street or the merchants whose stores open onto the sidewalk. They'll probably be enthusiastic about your idea and perhaps they'll help out with brooms you can use and trash cans for the litter you'll pick up.

But why stop at litter cleanup? Look carefully at the area you've adopted and see what would make it truly beautiful. You might plant flowers at the bases of the sidewalk trees or ground-cover plants on the sad stretch of ground between the sidewalk and the street. In some towns people have painted the fire hydrants in imaginative ways to look like clowns or firemen or fantasy animals. (Before you do this, check with the fire department to make sure it's okay.) Ask local merchants or homeowners if they'd be willing to buy the supplies—paint, flowers or bulbs, topsoil, or whatever is needed—and you'll supply the labor.

If walls along the sidewalk are continually defaced with ugly graffiti, talk with the building owners about painting a large wall mural there. This takes planning and careful work, but the results can be really impressive; often a gorgeous mural seems to make people feel happy and discourages them from messing up the wall it decorates.

It's a good idea to get your "Adopt a Public Land" project into the news. It will inspire other groups to follow your example, and it will let people know what great work you've been doing. Write to your local newspapers and radio and TV stations. Explain what you're doing and why you feel it's important. The more publicity you get, the more groups may jump on the bandwagon, and the whole community will benefit.

At the beginning of your cleanup project, be sure to take a "before" picture of your adopted area; later, when it's all cleaned up and beautified, you can take an "after" photo. The contrast will amaze everyone who sees it and will make a powerful point about the work you're doing. Seeing the difference you've made tells people how much a few determined kids can accomplish.

"Let's Bag It!"

What makes public places dirty is mostly litter. Everyone knows littering is bad, but sometimes it's hard to find a trash can when you need it. You can help prevent litter by making a set of litter bags to give as a gift. They are perfect for using in cars or attached to baby strollers, and you'll find lots of people who could use a set once you start thinking about it.

Ordinary paper lunch bags are perfect for these individual litter bags; they're not too big, and they're disposable when they're full. The idea is to provide a handy place to throw away small stuff like candy wrappers, used tissues and chew-

MAKING LITTER BAGS

ing gum, fast-food wrappers, even apple cores if they're not too drippy.

Use twelve bags to make your set. Punch holes near the top of each bag to make two parallel sets of holes. Then thread pieces of yarn or string through on each side; knot the ends to make handles for hanging the bag.

Now it's time to decorate your set of litter bags with markers or crayons or anything bright and colorful. You may want to write a slogan on each one, like "Let's Bag It!" But what about adding a joke or riddle to keep people cheerful and to make them pay attention to the litter bag's purpose? You can draw scenes of nice clean places, free of litter, or whatever you want; make each bag different to keep yourself from getting bored while you make them.

Your cousin who's just had a baby or your sister who's just gotten her first car will be delighted to have this useful and pretty gift.

September, first Sunday after Labor Day

National Grandparents Day

National Grandparents Day was founded by a woman from West Virginia named Marian McQuade. In 1973 she wrote to the governor of West Virginia, Arch Moore, asking him to announce a special day for grandparents and their grandchildren. Governor Moore liked the idea and he established a Grandparents Day for West Virginia.

Senator Jennings Randolph of West Virginia also got interested in the project. In 1978 the U.S. Senate passed his bill, which set National Grandparents Day as the first Sunday after Labor Day.

Since there is a Mother's Day and a Father's Day, it seems logical that there should be a Grandparents Day as well. People live such busy lives that sometimes it's hard to find time to spend with relatives. National Grandparents Day is the perfect time to visit your grandparents or to let them know by mail or phone how important they are in your life.

Some people feel there is often a special connection between grandparents and grandchildren. Grandparents aren't responsible for your everyday behavior or for all the details of taking care of you—taking you to the doctor and dentist, getting you new shoes when yours are outgrown, talking to your teachers when you have a problem in school, and all those other things that parents worry about. Your grandparents have already raised their own children, so in lots of ways they can just take it easy and have fun with you and your brothers and sisters.

Of course, many grandparents are retired, so they have more time than your mom and dad, who may have to go to work every day. Even if they're not retired, grandparents may be more willing to take time off to do things with you.

Your own grandparents may not look or act like the ones you see on TV commercials. Your grandma may be a skinny, energetic lady who loves to go bowling, instead of a plump white-haired woman who sits in her rocker when she's not baking cookies. And your grandpa may be an enthusiastic man who's so busy with your town's politics that he makes everyone else feel tired. But whatever they're like, your grandparents are sure to have a very special feeling for you, and they will be delighted to know that you feel the same way about them.

Did You Know . . . ?

Does your school have a Grandparents Day when kids' grandparents come and take part in special activities? Many schools have such events, and they're lots of fun for everyone—except for the kids whose grandparents don't live close enough to participate. These students often feel lonely and left out of the celebration.

Some schools have found a terrific way to solve this problem and make their Grandparents Day even better than before. They have asked older people in the neighborhood to be "foster" grandparents for kids whose own grandparents can't be there. Often the foster grandparents have the same situation in their own lives—their grandchildren live too far away to see them very often. So "adopting" one another for the day works out well for both grandparent and grandchild.

Why not ask your own school to try this idea on Grandparents Day? You never know—it might lead to a whole lot of brand-new friendships.

*

What gave Marian McQuade the idea for National Grandparents Day? She was thinking about elderly people she knew who were very lonely, and that led her to think about families getting together across the generations. Mrs. McQuade had worked with senior citizens for several years and had been a delegate from West Virginia to the White House Conference on Aging.

But Marian McQuade also had plenty of personal experience with grandparenting. She and her husband had fifteen children, and at last count they had thirty-eight grandchildren. That probably made her an expert on the subject.

CELEBRATE!

Roll Out the Fun

How about making something really special for your grandparents to celebrate National Grandparents Day? A handmade scroll is an easy project and it's guaranteed to give everyone a lot of laughs.

To make the scroll, you need plain white shelf paper. Sometimes this is difficult to find, because most stores carry only the vinyl-coated or plastic kind, and what you need is the plain paper kind. Try looking in dime stores or variety stores; even some large stationery stores may carry it. If you can't find shelf paper anywhere, you can tape several pieces of typing paper together end to end to make your scroll.

Next you will need a lot of magazines and advertising brochures that you can cut up. (The glossy paper that magazines are printed on works better than newspaper, which will smear.) You are going to cut out words and phrases from headlines and ads, and glue them to the scroll to form new sentences of your own. Use white glue to put the scroll together.

For example, suppose you want to make the sentence "Grandma loves to talk on the telephone." You might find the word "Grandma" or "Grandmother" in a headline about a woman who has a prize-winning garden. Cut that word out. Then you might find an ad that says someone "loves to fly" on a certain airline. Cut out the words "loves to" and put them next to "Grandma." Keep looking for the words and phrases you need until the scroll says what you want it to.

It doesn't matter if the sizes and styles of the letters are all different—that's part of the fun. And be on the lookout for extra phrases you can use—things like "In just 30 seconds" or "Wow!" or "Nine out of ten doctors say . . ." Add these to some of your sentences; you may be surprised at how funny they can sound. Pictures too can be part of your put-together message.

What should your scroll be about? Maybe it can describe the things you like to do with your grandparents—walking your dog, taking trips in the summer, going to ball games or the zoo. Maybe you'd rather find phrases that tell what you think is special about your grandparents—Grandpa's weird sense of humor, Grandma's willingness to help you learn to ski, or the way they both make you feel wanted and welcome when you have dinner at their house.

Or perhaps your scroll could tell about some special things that have happened since you were a baby—going to the park with Grandpa when you were only one and a half, feeding goldfish in a pond with Grandma when you were two, a "sleepover" at their house when you were three, and so on. Remembering these things while you're making your scroll reminds you all over again how lucky you are to have your grandparents around—and reading about your memories will make your grandparents feel very much loved.

When it's all finished and the glue is dry, you can sign your name and the date at the end. Cut off the extra shelf paper. (Hint: If you leave a lot of blank shelf paper at the end, you can add to this scroll next year or the year after if you want.) Now roll up your scroll and tie it with a ribbon. It's all ready to give to your grandparents with a lot of laughs and love.

Who's Who in This Picture?

Is there a whole bunch of old family photographs lying around in your house, or in your grandparents' house? If so, you and your grandparents can have a wonderful time getting them organized and putting them in an album. As you go, be sure to label each picture with the names of the people in it and the date it was taken. Grandma and Grandpa are probably the only people who really know who all those people are and when and where the photos were taken.

Perhaps there's a Cousin Bill you've never even heard of before; Grandma may have amazing stories to tell about him and his exciting life. Or maybe you'll find some baby pictures of your mom or dad; it can be startling to see how much he or she looks like you at that age, and Grandpa might be able to tell you lots of tales about the mischief your mom or dad got into years ago.

Looking at these family photos with your grandparents is a good way to learn fascinating information about your family and even about yourself. It strengthens the bonds between you and your grandparents and makes all of you feel a special sense of belonging.

International Day of Peace

In 1981 the General Assembly of the United Nations said that "the third Tuesday of September, the opening day of the regular sessions of the General Assembly, shall be officially proclaimed and observed as International Day of Peace and shall be devoted to commemorating and strengthening the ideals of peace both within and among all nations and peoples."

When the United Nations was started in 1945, representatives from the fifty-one countries who joined may have hoped that an International Day of Peace wouldn't be necessary by 1981 (the year the holiday was founded). In 1945 the world had just managed to bring World War II to an end. It had been a horrible conflict and millions of soldiers and civilians had died because of it. When it was over, people in many nations fervently hoped that we had all seen how stupid and awful wars could be. They hoped that an organization like the United Nations could help settle problems without bloodshed and destruction. In fact, the charter of the United Nations mentions peace as the first purpose of the organization. It says:

> We the peoples of the United Nations determined to save
> succeeding generations from the scourge of war, which
> twice in our lifetime has brought untold sorrow to man-
> kind, and . . .
> To practice tolerance and live together in peace with one
> another as good neighbors, and
> To unite our strength to maintain international peace
> and security, and
> To insure . . . that armed force shall not be used, save in
> the common interest, . . .
> have resolved to combine our efforts to accomplish these
> aims.

Unfortunately, the world has not been able to prevent wars from happening since the United Nations was begun in 1945. All over our planet, people have fought and killed one another in conflicts between countries and between opposing groups inside countries.

The United Nations is now composed of more than 160 countries. It has sent peacekeeping troops, made up of soldiers from several different countries that belong to the United Nations, to many places where wars were about to begin. Often these UN troops have helped to keep peace by forming a buffer zone between the enemies. The United Nations can also put economic pressure on countries who are at war by agreeing to cut off trade with that country until the fighting ends. And of course the United Nations provides a forum—a place where all the countries involved in a quarrel can sit down and talk about it in hopes of avoiding a war.

War is expensive, often wasting millions of dollars that could be spent on other things to improve people's lives. And war is tragic for everyone involved in it. Yet it seems that many world leaders still believe that fighting is the only way to settle their problems. Nevertheless, the efforts of the United Nations to make the world a more peaceful place have helped to keep wars from engulfing the whole world, and we can hope that peace will become the choice of more and more people as time goes on.

Did You Know . . . ?

The idea of an organization that would help preserve peace in the world was not new when the United Nations was formed in 1945. Earlier, during and after World War I, President Woodrow Wilson had envisioned a "general association of nations" that would make war a thing of the past. This organization was called the League of Nations, and President Wilson spent a great deal of time and energy figuring out how it should work and presenting his idea to the American public. The League of Nations, and the peace it could bring to the world, was what Wilson cared most about. Sadly, he became ill before he finished his speaking tour, and politicians who didn't want the United States to join the League of Nations continued to argue against Wilson's idea. So the United States did not join the other countries that organized the League of Nations; without the U.S., the League could not prevent the coming of World War II.

CELEBRATE!

What Does Peace Look Like?

A classroom display that symbolizes hope for peace all over the world is a wonderful way to celebrate this holiday. Think about the international symbols that mean "peace" to everyone. The dove and the olive branch have both represented peace through the centuries.

Make a peace wreath

Real olive branches may not be available, but you can use other kinds of flexible branches to make a peace wreath. Willows, ivy, and grapevine are good possibilities, or you may find thin branches of trees or bushes that will work well. Be

PEACE WREATH

sure you have permission before you cut any branches, and keep your eyes open for people doing their fall pruning.

The base of the wreath is a wire coat hanger stretched to make a circle; use the hook part to hang your wreath when it's finished. Wrap flexible branches around the hanger circle, or tie branches to the hanger with short pieces of cord. Keep adding branches until the wreath looks full and even all the way around.

Now add peace symbols to your wreath, attaching them with thread or cord. Dove shapes cut out of white felt make a perfect addition to the wreath; stuff a little cotton between two dove shapes and then glue the edges together to make a three-dimensional bird. Your wreath full of flying doves will express your hope for lasting worldwide peace.

Peace in the air

Why not also make a mobile for your class using peace symbols? Use wooden rods, stiff small branches, or pieces of wire coat hanger for the rods of the mobile; cut varying lengths of thread or fishing line to tie on the peace symbols so they appear to float in space.

Make more white doves out of felt or paper to fly on your mobile. Then add other elements to the design. Look up the word for "peace" in other languages; write these in fat connected letters on colored paper and cut out the whole word. Construction paper works fine, but you could also try origami paper or foil wrapping paper for a brighter look.

How about adding some peace symbols like the ones you see on T-shirts? Cut them out of paper too; if you draw the symbol on a circle of paper, be sure to draw it on both sides so it's always visible as it turns on the mobile.

When you put your mobile together, it may take some time to get everything to balance correctly so the arms stay level and the hanging pieces spin slowly in the breeze. But once it's finished, your mobile will be a reminder to everyone of the need for peaceful cooperation.

Speak Out for Peace

Sometimes it seems as though the opinions of ordinary people have no effect on decisions made by political leaders. It's easy to get discouraged and to feel that your voice is never heard on topics that you care deeply about. But it's not true! Any politician will tell you that elected officials care a lot about their constituents' views. They read the letters voters send to them and listen to their telephone calls. The more people talk about a particular issue, the more attention our political leaders will pay to it.

International Day of Peace is a good time to let your political leaders know how you feel about war and peace. Write a letter that explains your feelings and your ideas. Maybe you think that the money the United States spends on developing new weapons should be spent on schools or housing or cleaning up the environment. Or maybe you think that since kids are told by adults to settle their arguments without fighting, grown people who lead nations should be able to do the same thing. Perhaps you feel strongly that instead of shooting, countries should use their economic power to persuade a warlike nation to calm down.

Your letter doesn't have to be long—in fact, it's better if it's fairly short, so the person who receives it can read it quickly and get the main point you're making. Present your ideas as clearly as you can, and be sure to include your name and address so the person can write back.

Who should receive your letter about peace? Probably the people who have the power to make war and to decide whether to buy new weapons are good choices. You can send copies of your letter to the president of the United States, the two U.S. senators who represent your state, and the representative from your congressional district. If you want to send more copies, you might consider the secretary of state and the secretary of defense, and members of Congress who have influence on military matters, such as the chairperson of the Senate Armed Services Committee. Be sure to change the address and salutation on each copy of your letter—it makes a better impression if you call each person by his or her correct name and title!

Do you have friends who would also like to send letters about peace? If so, why not turn your "peace" letter into a chain letter? You can send copies of it to three friends, along with a cover letter to explain what it is. Ask each person to make seven copies of the "peace" letter. They will send the first four letters to the president, their two senators, and their representative. They will send the other three copies, with a note to explain the peace project, to three of their friends. Elected leaders will soon have a good idea of how you and a lot of people like you feel about the need for peace in the world.

Here are samples of a cover letter and a peace letter; you can copy them or write the letters in your own words.

Your address

Date

Dear [Friend's name],

Do you care about peace? Do you want to ask our political leaders to look for ways to solve problems without going to war? If so, please join the chain of people who want a peaceful world.

Make three copies of this letter; then make seven copies of the sample peace letter that is enclosed. You can add your own thoughts to it or change it if you want.

Send four copies of the peace letter to the following people: the president of the United States (The White House, 1600 Pennsylvania Avenue, Washington, DC 20500); the U.S. senators from your state (U.S. Senate, Washington, DC 20510); your representative (U.S. House of Representatives, Washington, DC 20515).

Send the other three peace letters, along with a copy of this cover letter, to three of your friends who want a peaceful world.

Let's hope that by next September, on the next International Day of Peace, we've made some progress toward ending war forever.

Yours truly,

[Your signature]

*

Your address

Date

Name of recipient
Address of recipient

Dear [Recipient's name]:

I am writing to tell you that I feel the most important issue today is making our country and our world a peaceful place to live. People tell children to talk over their disagreements and settle them without fighting; but if children are supposed to do this, why do adults still choose to settle their disagreements by fighting? I think adults should take their own advice and talk over their problems instead of going to war.

Almost every day the newspaper has articles about how expensive it is to buy new weapons and fighter planes and how much money it costs to send U.S. soldiers to fight wars. This money could be spent on things that would help the whole world, like cleaning up the environment or feeding people who are hungry.

I hope you agree with me that war is a stupid way to solve problems. Please try in every way you can to stop wars and make the world more peaceful.

Yours truly,
[Your signature]
Your typed name

Appendix

Here are some places you can write to ask for more information about various holidays.

Earth Day:
U.S. Environmental Protection Agency
Office of Public Affairs
401 M Street SW
Washington, DC 20460

International Children's Book Day:
USBBY Secretariat
c/o IRA
PO Box 8139
Newark, DE 19714

International Day of Peace:
United Nations
New York, NY 10017

International Lefthanders Day:
Lefthanders International
PO Box 8249
Topeka, KS 66608

Kwanzaa:
African-American Cultural Center
350 Masten Avenue
Buffalo, NY 14209

National Grandparents Day:
Marian McQuade, Founder
140 Main Street
Oak Hill, WV 25901

National Grouch Day:
Alan R. Miller
12281 Alexander Street
Clio, MI 48420

National Sandwich Day:
Public Relations
DowBrands Inc., Food Care Division
PO Box 78980
New Augusta, IN 46278

Public Lands Day:
Keep America Beautiful, Inc.
Mill River Plaza
9 W. Broad Street
Stamford, CT 06902

United Nations Day:
United Nations
New York, NY 10017

World Food Day:
National Coordinator
National Committee for World Food Day
1001 22nd Street NW
Washington, DC 20437

A book that lists lots of strange and wonderful holidays, and gives a little information about each one, can be found in the reference section of most libraries. It is called *Chase's Annual Events* and a new edition is published every year.

Selected Bibliography

Asterisks (*) indicate books of special interest to young readers.

Reference Works

Chase's Annual Events: The Day-By-Day Directory to 1992. Chicago: Contemporary Books, 1991.

Cohen, Hennig, and Coffin, Tristram Potter, eds. *The Folklore of American Holidays*. Detroit, MI: Gale Research, 1987.

Compton's Encyclopedia. Chicago: Compton's Learning Co., 1989.

The Concise Columbia Encyclopedia. New York: Columbia University Press, 1983.

Dunkling, Leslie. *A Dictionary of Days*. New York: Facts on File Publications, 1988.

Hatch, Jane M., comp. & ed. *The American Book of Days*. 3rd ed. New York: H. W. Wilson Co., 1978.

Myers, Robert J., and editors of Hallmark Cards. *Celebrations: The Complete Book of American Holidays*. Garden City, NY: Doubleday & Co., 1972.

Merit Student's Encyclopedia. New York: Macmillan Educational Co., 1987.

The New Book of Knowledge. Danbury, CT: Grolier, 1988.

Webster's New International Dictionary of the English Language. 2nd ed., unabridged. Springfield, MA: G. & C. Merriam Co., 1935.

The World Book Encyclopedia. Chicago: World Book, 1991.

228

Books

*Ahsan, M. M. *Muslim Festivals*. Vero Beach, FL: Rourke Enterprises, 1987.

*Arthur, Mildred. *Holidays of Legend: From New Year's to Christmas*. Irvington-on-Hudson, NY: Harvey House, 1971.

*Asian Cultural Center for Unesco. *Festivals in Asia*. New York: Kodansha International, 1975.

*———. *More Festivals in Asia*. New York: Kodansha International, 1975.

*Baldwin, Margaret. *Thanksgiving: A First Book*. New York: Franklin Watts, 1983.

*Barkin, Carol, and James, Elizabeth. *Happy Thanksgiving!* New York: Lothrop, Lee & Shepard Books, 1987.

*———. *Happy Valentine's Day!* New York: Lothrop, Lee & Shepard Books, 1988.

*———. *The Scary Halloween Costume Book*. New York: Lothrop, Lee & Shepard Books, 1983.

*Barth, Edna. *Hearts, Cupids, and Red Roses: The Story of the Valentine Symbols*. New York: Clarion Books, 1982.

*———. *Shamrocks, Harps, and Shillelaghs: The Story of the St. Patrick's Day Symbols*. New York: Clarion Books, 1977.

*———. *Turkeys, Pilgrims, and Indian Corn: The Story of the Thanksgiving Symbols*. New York: Clarion Books, 1975.

*———. *Witches, Pumpkins, and Grinning Ghosts: The Story of the Halloween Symbols*. New York: Clarion Books, 1972.

*Brown, Tricia. *Chinese New Year*. New York: Henry Holt & Co., 1987.

Burland, Cottie. *North American Indian Mythology*. New York: Peter Bedrick Books, 1985.

*Burnett, Bernice. *Holidays: A First Reference Book*. New York: Franklin Watts, 1983.

Burns, Marilyn. *This Book Is About Time*. Boston: Little, Brown & Co., 1978.

*Cantwell, Mary. *St. Patrick's Day*. New York: Thomas Y. Crowell Co., 1967.

Cavendish, Richard. *The Great Religions*. New York: Arco Publishing Co., 1980.

*Cheng, Hou-tien. *The Chinese New Year*. New York: Holt, Rinehart & Winston, 1976.

Chute, Marchette. *The First Liberty: A History of the Right to Vote in America, 1619-1850*. New York: E. P. Dutton & Co., 1969.

Coolidge, Olivia. *Women's Rights: The Suffrage Movement in America, 1848-1920*. New York: E. P. Dutton & Co., 1966.

*Corbin, Carole Lynn. *The Right to Vote*. New York: Franklin Watts, 1985.

*Dobler, Lavinia. *Customs and Holidays Around the World*. New York: Fleet Publishing Corp., 1962.

*Domnitz, Myer. *Judaism*. New York: Bookwright Press, 1986.

*DowBrands. *Bread Winners: A Cookbook for Kids Featuring "America's Favorite Sandwiches."* New Augusta, IN: DowBrands, n.d.

*DowBrands/Instructor Publications. *Two Slices of Bread and a Whole Lot More*. New Augusta, IN: DowBrands, n.d.

*Editorial Staff of *Life*. *The World's Great Religions*. New York: Simon & Schuster, 1958.

Fincher, Jack. *Sinister People*. New York: G.P. Putnam, 1977.

Fuson, Robert H., trans. *The Log of Christopher Columbus*. Camden, ME: International Marine Publishing Co., 1987.

*Gaer, Joseph. *Holidays Around the World*. Boston: Little, Brown & Co., 1953.

*Giblin, James Cross. *Fireworks, Picnics and Flags*. New York: Clarion Books, 1983.

*Greene, Carol. *Holidays Around the World*. Chicago: Children's Press, 1982.

*Grigoli, Valerie. *Patriotic Holidays and Celebrations: A First Book*. New York: Franklin Watts, 1985.

Hardon, John A., S.J. *Religions of the World*. Mahwah, NJ: The Newman Press, 1963.

*Harris, Jacqueline L. *Martin Luther King, Jr*. New York: Franklin Watts, 1983.

*Haskins, James. *Religions*. Philadelphia: J. B. Lippincott Co., 1973.

*Heinrichs, Ann. *America the Beautiful: Wyoming*. Chicago: Children's Press, 1992.

*Humble, Richard, and editors of Time-Life Books. *The Seafarers*. New York: Time-Life Books, 1978.

Iacopi, Robert L. *Look to the Mountain Top*. San Jose, CA: Gousha Publications, 1972.

Ickis, Margaret. *The Book of Festival Holidays*. New York: Dodd, Mead & Co., 1964.

*Irwin, Constance. *Strange Footprints on the Land: Vikings in America*. New York: Harper & Row, 1980.

*Janeway, Elizabeth. *The Vikings*. New York: Random House, 1951.

*Kanitkar, V. P. *Hinduism*. New York: Bookwright Press, 1986.

Keep America Beautiful. *Changing Attitudes in American Communities*. Stamford, CT: Keep America Beautiful, n.d.

Keep America Beautiful/Take Pride in America. *Preserving Our National Heritage: A Stewardship Guide for Public Resources*. N.p., n.d.

*Kelley, Emily. *Happy New Year*. Minneapolis, MN: Carolrhoda Books, 1984.

Kimball, Yeffe, and Anderson, Jean. *The Art of American Indian Cooking*. New York: Doubleday & Co., 1965.

*Kraske, Robert. *The Story of the Dictionary*. New York: Harcourt Brace Jovanovich, 1975.

*Leon, George deLucenay. *Explorers of the Americas Before Columbus*. New York: Franklin Watts, 1979.

*Le Sueur, Meridel. *Little Brother of the Wilderness: The Story of Johnny Appleseed*. Duluth, MN: Holy Cow! Press, 1987.

*Limburg, Peter R. *Weird! The Complete Book of Halloween Words*. New York: Bradbury Press, 1989.

*Lomask, Milton. *Great Lives: Exploration*. New York: Charles Scribner's Sons, 1988.

*Manning-Saunders, Ruth. *Festivals*. New York: E. P. Dutton & Co., 1973.

*McKey, Don. *Martin Luther King, Jr.* New York: G. P. Putnam's Sons, 1969.

*McSpadden, J. Walker. *The Book of Holidays*. T. Y. Crowell Co., 1958.

*Meltzer, Milton. *Columbus and the World Around Him*. New York: Franklin Watts, 1990.

*——. *George Washington and the Birth of Our Nation*. Franklin Watts, 1986.

*Mooser, Stephen. *Monster Fun*. New York: Julian Messner, 1979.

*Patrick, Diane. *Martin Luther King, Jr.: A First Book*. New York: Franklin Watts, 1990.

*Patterson, Lillie. *Martin Luther King, Jr. and the Freedom Movement*. New York: Facts on File, 1989.

*Phelan, Mary Kay. *Mother's Day*. New York: T. Y. Crowell Co., 1965.

*Pittman, Margaret Brown. *The Mystery of Who Discovered the Americas*. New York: Contemporary Perspectives, 1979.

*Porter, A. P. *Kwanzaa*. Minneapolis, MN: Carolrhoda Books, 1991.

*Quayle, Louise. *Martin Luther King, Jr.: Dreams for a Nation*. New York: Fawcett Columbine, 1989.

*Rice, Edward. *The Five Great Religions*. New York: Four Winds Press, 1973.

*Sarnoff, Jane, and Ruffins, Reynold. *Light the Candles! Beat the Drums! A Book of Holidays*. New York: Charles Scribner's Sons, 1979.

Schauffler, Robert Haven. *Memorial Day*. New York: Dodd, Mead & Co., 1911, 1930.

*Scott, Geoffrey. *Memorial Day*. Minneapolis, MN: Carolrhoda Books, 1983.

Seeds of Change: A Guide for Young People. Washington, DC: National Museum of Natural History, Smithsonian Institution, n.d.

*Seeger, Elizabeth. *Eastern Religions*. New York: T. Y. Crowell Co., 1973.

*Showers, Paul. *Indian Festivals*. New York: T. Y. Crowell Co., 1969.

*Silverstein, Alvin and Virginia. *The Story of Your Hand*. New York: G. P. Putnam's Sons, 1985.

*Singh, Daljit, and Smith, Angela. *The Sikh World*. Morristown, NJ: Silver Burdett Co., 1985.

*Snelling, John. *Buddhism*. New York: Bookwright Press, 1986.

*Soule, Gardner. *Christopher Columbus*. New York: Franklin Watts, 1988.

*Stevenson, Janet. *Women's Rights*. New York: Franklin Watts, 1972.

United Nations. *Visitors' Guide: United Nations*. New York: United Nations, 1988.

United States Environmental Protection Agency. *Earth Day 1990*. Washington, DC: U.S. Environmental Protection Agency, 1990.

———. *You Can Make a Difference*. Washington, DC: U.S. Environmental Protection Agency, 1990.

———. *Earth Day Recollection*. Washington, DC: U.S. Environmental Protection Agency, 1990.

*Van Straalen, Alice. *The Book of Holidays Around the World*. New York: E. P. Dutton & Co., 1986.

White, David. *The Great Book of Flags*. Vero Beach, FL: Rourke Enterprises, 1989.

Wright, Lawrence. *Clockwork Man: The Story of Time, Its Origins, Its Uses, Its Tyranny*. New York: Horizon Press, 1969.

Articles

Aberle, Jean. "Goodies for Goblins." *Diabetes Today* (September 1990): 45-48.

Associated Press. "Before There Were Daytimers." *Los Angeles Times* (December 31, 1992): E1.

Aubry, Erin J. "Cultural Legacy." *Los Angeles Times* (December 27, 1992): J3.

Bernstein, Richard. "Nonsexist Dictionary Spells Out Rudeness." *New York Times* (June 11, 1991): C13.

Bizzarro, Salvatore. "The Legacy of Columbus." *Colorado College Bulletin* (October 1992): 3.

Coontz, Stephanie. "Mothers in Arms." *New York Times* (May 10, 1992): A19.

Copage, Eric V. "The Seven Days of Kwanzaa." *New York Times* (December 1, 1991): Travel section, 18.

Doheny, Kathleen, "Junior E-Men on Patrol." *Los Angeles Times* (June 22, 1990): E1.

Eppinger, Dr. Paul. "YES: Holiday a Symbol of Basic Principles of United States." *Phoenix Gazette* (October 27, 1992): A11.

Foote, Timothy. "Where Columbus Was Coming From." *Smithsonian* (December 1991): 28-41.

"1492–1992: When Worlds Collide: How Columbus's Voyages Transformed Both East and West." *Newsweek,* Columbus Special Issue: A Joint Project with the Smithsonian's Natural History Exhibit "Seeds of Change" (Fall/Winter 1991).

" 'Ghosts' Curb Business Action in Singapore." *Los Angeles Times* (August 17, 1992): D3.

Gordon, Larry. "Charting New Courses in Teaching About Columbus." *Los Angeles Times* (December 26, 1991): A1.

Hillinger, Charles. "Flag Day is Biggest Day at Holiday's Birthplace." *Los Angeles Times* (June 15, 1987): 16.

Kristof, Nicholas D. "For Better or Worse, Year of Rooster Dawns." *New York Times* (January 24, 1993): 8.

Lara, Adair. "The Right Way to Do Halloween." *Redbook* (October 1992): 184.

McCarthy, Abigail. "As Islam Grows, It Remains Misunderstood." *Los Angeles Times* (February 20, 1993): B5.

Mehren, Elizabeth. "Ports in the Storm." *Los Angeles Times* (November 25, 1992): E1.

Ponte, Lowell. "What's Right About Being Left-Handed?" *Reader's Digest* (July 1988): 133-35.

Reid, Alastair. "Waiting for Columbus." *New Yorker* (February 24, 1992): 57-75.

Rosenberg, Merri. "Saving the Earth for More Than One Day." *New York Times* (May 17, 1992): Westchester section, 5.

Seay, Gina. "Kwanzaa Fetes Black Heritage." *Houston Chronicle* (December 23, 1990): 1G.

Simonds, Nina. "Year of the Rooster." *Los Angeles Times* (January 21, 1993): H1.

"Town Begins 65 Days of Darkness." *Los Angeles Times* (November 19, 1992).

Wilford, John Noble. "Dominican Bluff Yields Columbus's First Colony." *New York Times* (November 27, 1990): C1.

———. "Norsemen in America Flourished, Then Faded." *New York Times* (July 7, 1992): C1.

Williams, Lena. "In Blacks' Homes, the Christmas and Kwanzaa Spirits Meet." *New York Times* (December 20, 1990): C6.

Zinsser, William. "I Realized Her Tears Were Becoming Part of the Memorial." *Smithsonian* (September 1991): 32-43.

Index